Biochemistry

Richard Harwood

Series editor: Brian Ratcliff

CAMBRIDGE
UNIVERSITY PRESS

PUBLISHED BY THE PRESS SYNDICATE OF THE UNIVERSITY OF CAMBRIDGE
The Pitt Building, Trumpington Street, Cambridge, United Kingdom

CAMBRIDGE UNIVERSITY PRESS
The Edinburgh Building, Cambridge CB2 2RU, UK
40 West 20th Street, New York, NY 10011-4211, USA
477 Williamstown Road, Port Melbourne, VIC 3207, Australia
Ruiz de Alarcón 13, 28014 Madrid, Spain
Dock House, The Waterfront, Cape Town 8001, South Africa

http://www.cambridge.org

First published 2002
Reprinted 2002

Printed in the United Kingdom at the University Press, Cambridge

Typeface Swift   *System* QuarkXPress®

A catalogue record for this book is available from the British Library

ISBN 0 521 79751 9 paperback

Produced by Gecko Ltd, Bicester, Oxon

Front cover photograph: False-colour scanning electron micrograph of spongy
bone; Science Photo Library

Contents

Introduction

Cambridge Advanced Sciences

The *Cambridge Advanced Sciences* series has been developed to meet the demands of all the new AS and A level science examinations. In particular, it has been endorsed by OCR as providing complete coverage of their specifications. The AS material is presented as a single text for each of biology, chemistry and physics. Material for the A2 year comprises six books in each subject: one of core material and one for each option. Some material has been drawn from the existing *Cambridge Modular Sciences* books; however, many parts are entirely new.

During the development of this series, the opportunity has been taken to improve the design, and a complete and thorough new writing and editing process has been applied. Much more material is now presented in colour. Although the existing *Cambridge Modular Sciences* texts do cover most of the new specifications, the *Cambridge Advanced Sciences* books cover every OCR learning objective in detail. They are the key to success in the new AS and A level examinations.

OCR is one of the three unitary awarding bodies offering the full range of academic and vocational qualifications in the UK. For full details of the new specifications, please contact OCR:

OCR, 1 Hills Rd, Cambridge CB1 2EU
Tel: 01223 553311

The presentation of units

You will find that the books in this series use a bracketed convention in the presentation of units within tables and on graph axes. For example, ionisation energies of $1000\,kJ\,mol^{-1}$ and $2000\,kJ\,mol^{-1}$ will be represented in this way:

Measurement	Ionisation energy ($kJ\,mol^{-1}$)
1	1000
2	2000

OCR examination papers use the solidus as a convention, thus:

Measurement	Ionisation energy / $kJ\,mol^{-1}$
1	1000
2	2000

Any numbers appearing in brackets with the units, for example ($10^{-5}\,mol\,dm^{-3}\,s^{-1}$), should be treated in exactly the same way as when preceded by the solidus, /$10^{-5}\,mol\,dm^{-3}\,s^{-1}$.

Biochemistry – an A2 option text

Biochemistry contains everything needed to cover the A2 option of the same name. It is a brand new text which has been written specifically with the new OCR specification in mind. A specialised glossary of terms is included, linked to the main text via the index. There is also an appendix of biological terms to assist non-biologists in their study of biochemistry. Students are advised to consult a GCSE textbook, such as Jones & Jones Biology (ISBN 0 521 45618 5) for further information regarding biological background and definitions.

The book is divided into seven chapters. The first is a biological prologue and the following five chapters correspond to the module sections of the same names.

This module builds upon, and presupposes knowledge of, material in *Chemistry 1*, It is also assumed that students have studied the Chains, Rings & Spectroscopy module which is covered in *Chemistry 2*.

Acknowledgements

1.1a, b, 1.4a, NASA/Science Photo Library; 1.3, Fred McConnaughey/Science Photo Library; 1.4b, Mount Stromlo and Siding Spring Observatories/Science Photo Library; 2.1a, 6.14b, CNRI/Science Photo Library; 2.1b, Ken Eward/Science Photo Library; 2.5, 5.4, © Neil Thompson; 2.19, © Ida Cook; 2.20, © NHF Hairdressing Training School; 3.1, PDB ID:1BIC; 3.17, CC Studio/Science Photo Library; 4.2, © EMPICS; 4.6, 5.23, © Maximilian Stock; 4.20, 5.18b, Andrew Syred/Science Photo Library; 4.22, © Geoff Jones; 4.23, Dr Don Fawcett/Science Photo Library; 4.24, Alvey & Towers; 4.26, Alan Bedding Images; 5.18, 5.19, NIBSC/Science Photo Library; 5.20, Microfield Scientific Ltd/Science Photo Library; 5.21, QUEST/Science Photo Library; 6.1, A Barrington Brown/Science Photo Library; 6.2a, Maximilian Stock Ltd/Science Photo Library; 6.2b, Science Source/Science Photo Library; 6.3, Laguna Design/Science Photo Library; 6.14a, Eye of Science/ Science Photo Library; 6.14c, © Biophoto Associates

CHAPTER 1

Prologue 序幕, 开场白,

The origin of life

How did life begin? A Martian meteorite found in Egypt has been studied by scientists from NASA. They claim to have found fossilised traces of early life inside the meteorite (*figure 1.1*). An ice-covered ocean has been discovered on Europa, one of the moons of Jupiter, and life could have evolved under this cover of ice. Discoveries such as these make headline news, showing our fascination with the origins of life.

During the twentieth century, scientists proposed a number of different ways in which life on Earth could have originated.

● **Figure 1.1** Is there life on Mars? **a** This meteorite from Mars, found in Egypt, contains microscopic structures, **b**, that look similar to bacteria found on Earth.

■ Lightning could have provided the energy to form simple biological molecules from the mixture of water, hydrogen, methane and ammonia that existed on Earth 4000 million years ago. A process similar to this has been carried out in the laboratory (*figure 1.2*).

■ Deep-sea thermal vents provide both energy and an environment rich in minerals, methane, carbon monoxide, ammonia and hydrogen sulphide. Biological molecules can be synthesised under these conditions (*figure 1.3*).

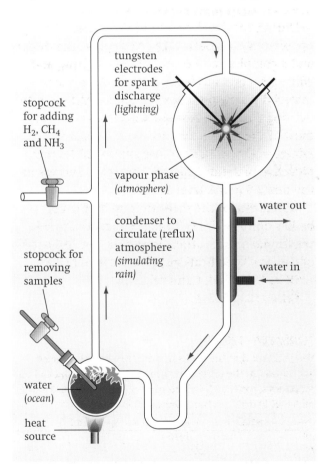

● **Figure 1.2** Stanley Miller, a graduate student at the University of Chicago, conducted an important experiment in the early 1950s. Starting from simple molecules, he managed to make many of the amino acids that are found in all proteins. The apparatus he used attempted to mimic the conditions found on the early Earth.

● **Figure 1.3** Deep ocean vents – a possible starting point for life? The water is chemically rich and the energy needed to drive chemical reactions would be provided by the high temperatures (up to 380 °C).

■ Complex biological molecules have been detected in space. Could biologically important molecules have been formed in the vast molecular clouds of the galaxies? These molecules could then have fallen to Earth with meteorites and 'seeded' the early Earth.

On February 7th 1999 NASA launched the spacecraft *Stardust* (figure 1.4). *Stardust* is planned to pass about 100 km in front of the comet Wild 2 on January 2nd 2004, collecting dust and volatile compounds from the gases and dust at the head of the comet, before returning to Earth in January 2006. The results of this mission may shed light on whether space debris has been involved in the origin of life on Earth.

Ideas on the origins of life remain speculative. However, all of these ideas share one unifying theme. This theme is that life, at its most basic level, is the chemistry of a surprisingly limited number of organic compounds and inorganic ions undergoing carefully controlled reactions in just one solvent – water. The study of life from this perspective has revolutionised our view of ourselves and led to some of the most astounding scientific discoveries and advances of modern times. This branch of science has become known as **biochemistry**.

Water – life's solvent

What makes water so vital for life? Animals and plants living in 'normal' environments cannot survive without a regular supply of water. Life, as we know it, could never have evolved without

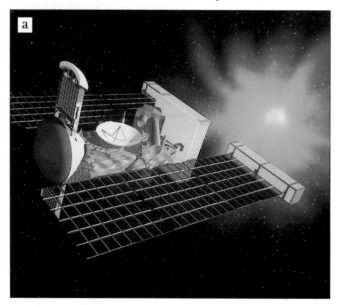

● **Figure 1.4 a** The spacecraft *Stardust* – on its way to the comet Wild 2 to collect samples of interstellar gas and dust. **b** Gaseous pillars in the Eagle nebula, showing 'star factories' surrounded by huge clouds of cosmic dust.

water. Some of the most significant biological roles of water are summarised in *figure 1.5*.

Hydrogen bonding

Perhaps the most remarkable property of water is that it is liquid at the normal temperatures found on Earth. Because of its small molecular mass, water should be a gas – just like the similar molecules methane (CH_4) and hydrogen sulphide (H_2S). The reason that water is not a gas is that it contains **hydrogen bonding** (see *Chemistry 1*, chapter 3).

The electrons present in the covalent bond between an oxygen atom and a hydrogen atom in a water molecule are shared unequally because oxygen is a highly electronegative atom. The oxygen atom draws the bonding electrons towards itself and so gains a partial negative charge. Because of this, the hydrogen atom is left with a partial positive charge and the hydrogen–oxygen bond becomes polarised. Water is a polar molecule (*figure 1.6*).

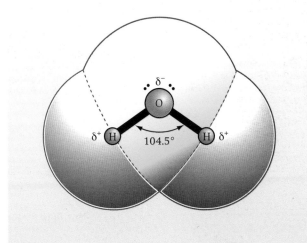

● **Figure 1.6** The polarised nature of the oxygen–hydrogen bond in a water molecule.

These partial positive and negative charges provide a force that attracts water molecules together. A hydrogen atom on one water molecule is attracted to the oxygen atom of another, forming a hydrogen bond (*figure 1.7*). Hydrogen bonds are much weaker than the covalent bonds within molecules but are stronger than the intermolecular **van der Waals' forces** that occur between molecules (see *Box 1A*, overleaf, and *Chemistry 1*, chapter 3). The existence of hydrogen bonding results in water having a higher than expected boiling point,

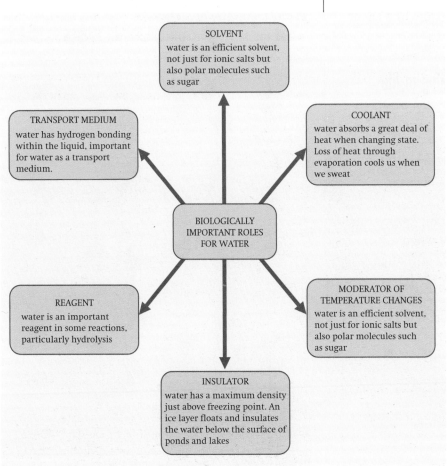

● **Figure 1.5** A summary of the biologically important roles of water.

SOLVENT
water is an efficient solvent, not just for ionic salts but also polar molecules such as sugar

TRANSPORT MEDIUM
water has hydrogen bonding within the liquid, important for water as a transport medium.

COOLANT
water absorbs a great deal of heat when changing state. Loss of heat through evaporation cools us when we sweat

BIOLOGICALLY IMPORTANT ROLES FOR WATER

REAGENT
water is an important reagent in some reactions, particularly hydrolysis

MODERATOR OF TEMPERATURE CHANGES
water is an efficient solvent, not just for ionic salts but also polar molecules such as sugar

INSULATOR
water has a maximum density just above freezing point. An ice layer floats and insulates the water below the surface of ponds and lakes

● **Figure 1.7** Hydrogen bonding between water molecules.

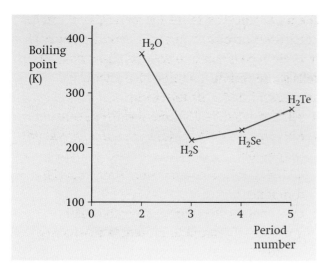

• **Figure 1.8** Boiling points of Group VI hydrides. Water has an unusually high boiling point because of hydrogen bonding.

compared with other hydrides of Group VI (H_2S, H_2Se and H_2Te) (*figure 1.8*).

The polar nature of water allows ionic compounds to dissolve in water. Hydrogen bonding also means that organic molecules containing polar groups are soluble in water. This is the case for many biological molecules, and so water is an ideal solvent.

The importance of hydrogen bonding to life

There are three properties of hydrogen bonds that make them important for life.
- They are transient – they are made and broken relatively easily.
- They have direction – the atoms involved become aligned.
- They have specificity – only certain groups can take part. Hydrogen bonds form when a hydrogen atom attached to an O or N atom bonds to another O or N atom.

Water illustrates these properties. Liquid water consists of a network of hydrogen-bonded molecules, but an individual hydrogen bond lasts

Box 1A Bond enthalpies
Bond enthalpies are a measure of the strength of a bond. Average values for a typical covalent bond, a hydrogen bond in water and a typical van der Waals' force are:
- C–C bond, $+346 \, kJ \, mol^{-1}$
- hydrogen bond in water, $+22 \, kJ \, mol^{-1}$
- van der Waals' force in neon, $+2 \, kJ \, mol^{-1}$.

for no more than a trillionth of a second. Water molecules are constantly jostling with each other, moving past each other, breaking and re-making hydrogen bonds with different molecules.

The structure of ice illustrates that hydrogen bonds have direction. In ice, hydrogen bonds contribute to the 'diamond-like' tetrahedral arrangement of the atoms in the lattice (*figure 1.9*). The three atoms involved in a hydrogen bond lie in a straight line.

The properties of hydrogen bonds are also of enormous importance in the way they affect biological molecules.
- The structures of many biological molecules are controlled in part by hydrogen bonding between different parts of their structure. The secondary structure of proteins (see chapter 2) and base pairing in DNA (see chapter 6) are two important features dependent on hydrogen bonding.
- The alignment, direction and weakness of hydrogen bonds help enzymes to catalyse reactions of biological molecules (see chapter 3).
- The solubility of all biological molecules is affected by their ability to form hydrogen bonds.

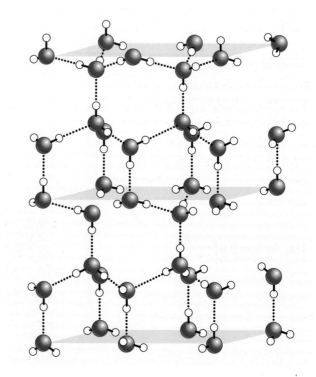

• **Figure 1.9** Hydrogen bonding in ice. The 'open' structure of ice is a consequence of hydrogen bonding. As a result, the density of ice (solid) is less than that of water (liquid).

- The positioning of phosphoglycerides in cell membranes involves polar regions of molecules interacting with water through hydrogen bonding (see chapter 5).

Although hydrogen bonds are very important, dipole–dipole forces and van der Waals' forces are also significant in determining the properties of biological compounds.

pH and buffers

Interactions between ionic groups and groups capable of hydrogen bonding are vital to the correct functioning of biological molecules. These interactions are dependent on pH, and the pH of any biochemical environment must be carefully controlled. The blood of a healthy person is slightly alkaline (pH 7.4) and should not vary by more than 0.1 in either direction.

- If the pH falls below 7.3, the blood can no longer efficiently take up and carry away the carbon dioxide produced in cells.
- A drop in pH to 6.8, as can happen in diabetes, may lead to coma and death.
- If the pH rises above 7.7, the carbon dioxide in the bloodstream cannot be effectively released to the lungs.

To ensure that the pH remains finely tuned, a system of pH control known as **buffering** exists in the blood (see *Chemistry 2*, chapter 14). In blood this buffer system is based on the hydrogencarbonate ion. Similar systems, based on hydrogencarbonate or phosphate ions, regulate the pH of other environments within living organisms.

Life is cellular

All living organisms (this includes animals, plants and bacteria) are made up of basic units called **cells**. Cells are enclosed collections of molecules and structures within a **cell membrane** (see chapter 5 for a discussion of the structure of cell membranes). Within a cell, the chemical processes of life (or metabolism) can be precisely controlled. Cells vary considerably both in their appearance and function. However, all cells share certain common characteristics, among which are the following:

- cells arise by the division of existing cells;
- cells contain DNA as their genetic material (see chapter 6);
- all living cells contain water as an essential component;
- cells contain ribosomes – the molecular 'machines' involved in protein synthesis (see chapter 6).

The structures of life

There are relatively few types of compounds involved in life. The main classes of compounds that we will be studying in later chapters are:

- proteins (in particular, enzymes);
- carbohydrates;
- lipids;
- nucleic acids (DNA and RNA).

The chemical components of a typical bacterial cell are summarised in *figure 1.10* (see also *figure 2.2* on page 8 for a similar summary for an adult human male).

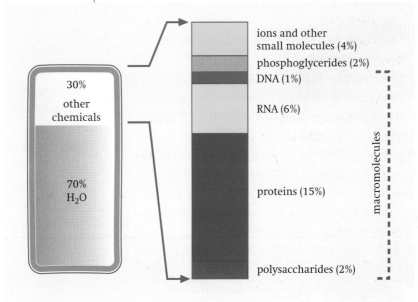

● **Figure 1.10** A summary of the chemical components of a bacterial cell.

30% other chemicals

70% H₂O

ions and other small molecules (4%)
phosphoglycerides (2%)
DNA (1%)
RNA (6%)
proteins (15%)
polysaccharides (2%)
macromolecules

Proteins (chapter 2)

Proteins are an extremely important and varied class of molecule. They are condensation polymers synthesised from amino acid monomer units (see *Chemistry 2*, chapter 5). Their main biological functions are:

- as structural molecules, adding strength and/or flexibility to tissues such as bone and hair;
- as enzymes, controlling the reactions within cells (see below and chapter 3);
- as antibodies and hormones;
- as components of cell membranes (see chapter 5).

Enzymes (chapter 3)

Enzymes are proteins that act as biological catalysts. Without them, the reactions that make life possible would be too slow for life to exist. Enzymes:

- show great specificity, only catalysing reactions involving a particular molecule or class of molecule;
- control the specificity of a reaction in such a way as to produce 'clean' reactions with very few side-products;
- are extremely sensitive to changes in conditions such as temperature and pH;
- are extremely sensitive to the presence of certain molecules known as inhibitors and cofactors;
- are far more efficient than the inorganic catalysts used in the chemical industry.

Carbohydrates (chapter 4)

Carbohydrates are a group of structurally related molecules that provide plants and animals with energy; that is they act as a fuel. They are made of only carbon, hydrogen and oxygen. Carbohydrates exist as:

- **monosaccharides** – simple sugar molecules, with the general formula $(CH_2O)_n$, which provide instant-access energy for plants and animals and act as structural units of many polysaccharides (see below);
- **disaccharides** – dimers of monosaccharides, which function as transport molecules for monosaccharides in organisms and as structural units in some polysaccharides;
- **polysaccharides** – condensation polymers of monosaccharides or disaccharides used for energy storage and as structural components of cells.

Lipids (chapter 5)

Lipids play essential roles in cell structure and metabolism. They are grouped together because they are insoluble in water. Lipids include the following molecular types: triglycerides, phosphoglycerides and steroids.

- **Triglycerides** occur in animal fats, which are solid at room temperature, and vegetable oils, which are liquid at room temperature. Fats and oils are the major stores of metabolic energy in plants and animals.
- **Phosphoglycerides** are important constituents of cell membranes. In water, phosphoglycerides group together to form a double layer (a bilayer), which is the fundamental structure of cell membranes.
- **Steroids** are a series of biologically important molecules. Examples are cholesterol, testosterone, oestrogen and cortisone. However, steroids will not be discussed in detail in this book.

Nucleic acids (chapter 6)

The nucleic acid DNA (**deoxyribonucleic acid**) carries all of an organism's genetic information at the molecular level. DNA:

- is a self-replicating molecule, that is it can copy itself exactly;
- is capable of passing genetic information from one generation to the next;
- contains the information needed to synthesise proteins.

The other structurally similar nucleic acid RNA (**ribonucleic acid**) is also involved in the synthesis of proteins.

The discovery of the structure of DNA is generally thought to be the greatest scientific achievement of the last century and has opened up vast new areas of research that impact our lives in a variety of ways.

CHAPTER 2

Amino acids and proteins

By the end of this chapter you should be able to:

1 explain the term *primary structure of proteins*;

2 describe the major features of the *secondary structure* of proteins as α-helix and β-pleated sheet and understand the stabilisation of these structures by hydrogen bonding;

3 state the importance of the *tertiary structure* in proteins, and explain the stabilisation of the tertiary structure by interactions between the R groups in the amino acid residues (ionic linkages, disulphide bridges, hydrogen bonds and instantaneous dipole-induced dipole forces (van der Waals' forces);

4 describe the *quaternary structure* of proteins, for example haemoglobin, including the role of Fe^{2+} ions in the functioning of this protein;

5 explain the *denaturation* of proteins by heavy metal ions, extremes of temperature and pH changes.

Proteins are large and complex biological polymers. For instance, the haemoglobin in your red blood cells has the formula $C_{2952}H_{4664}O_{832}N_{812}S_8Fe_4$ and a molecular mass of about 65 000 (*figure 2.1*). Until the 1930s, proteins were thought not to have an organised structure. However, recent investigations have shown that proteins do have a very ordered structure. As our understanding of the structure of proteins has increased, so too has the realisation that proteins are involved in virtually every biological process. (The structure of haemoglobin is discussed later in this chapter.)

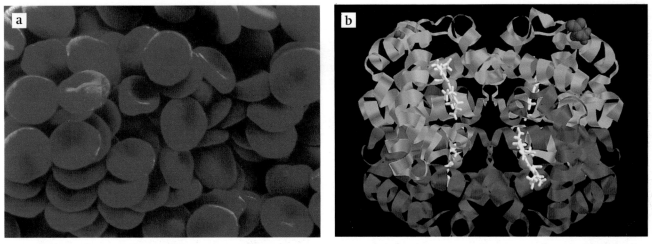

● **Figure 2.1 a** Human red blood cells (× 2000) are highly specialised cells whose function is to transport oxygen in the blood – haemoglobin is the protein that carries the oxygen. **b** This computer-generated model of haemoglobin shows the polypeptide subunits of haemoglobin as coiled ribbons (the α-chains are blue, the β-chains are yellow). Each subunit carries a haem group (white), to which the oxygen binds, via Fe^{2+} ions. See page 17 for more details.

Proteins make up approximately 18% of the mass of an average person (*figure 2.2*). Many proteins, such as antibodies, enzymes and haemoglobin, are water-soluble molecules and can be transported easily within and between cells and tissues. Others, such as collagen and keratin, are insoluble and form very tough, stable structures. Some proteins and their functions are listed in *table 2.1*.

Amino acids – the building blocks of proteins

Common features of amino acids

Amino acids are important organic molecules because they are used by living organisms as the building blocks of proteins (see *Chemistry 2*, chapter 5). In nature, protein chains are synthesised from a selection of just 20 amino acids. Nineteen of these amino acids contain the same two functional groups – a carboxylic acid group (–COOH) and a primary amino group (–NH$_2$). The amino acid proline is

Protein	Function	Where found
myosin	muscle contraction	muscle tissue
actin	muscle contraction	muscle tissue
pepsin	digestive enzyme, breaks down food	stomach
chymotrypsin	digestive enzyme, breaks down food	small intestine
catalase	oxidative enzyme, removes hydrogen peroxide that would damage tissues	liver, kidney, blood
insulin	hormone, enables use of glucose for energy	blood, pancreas
immunoglobulins	antibodies	blood, lymph
collagen	structural, gives strength and elasticity	skin, tendon
keratin	structural	hair and nails
haemoglobin	transport of oxygen between lungs and rest of the body	blood
ferritin	storage of iron	bone marrow, liver, spleen

● **Table 2.1** Some proteins and their functions in the human body.

the exception in that it is a cyclic compound and contains a secondary amino group instead of a primary amino group. However, the 20 molecules all have one feature in common: the two functional groups are both attached to the same carbon atom (*figure 2.3*). This carbon atom is then also attached to a hydrogen atom and a side-chain, shown as –R in *figure 2.3*.

When naming organic acids systematically, the carbon atom of the acid group is always counted as the first in the structure. This means that, for the amino acids that make up proteins, the amino group is always attached to the second carbon atom (C-2), the one immediately adjacent to the carboxylic acid group. This carbon atom is also known as the α-carbon. All the amino acids in proteins are therefore 2-amino acids – and are more usually known as **α-amino acids**. However, it is usual to refer to them merely as 'amino acids', with the 'α-' assumed.

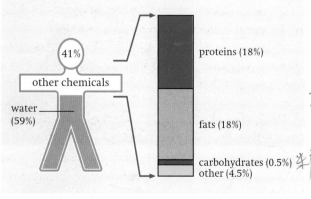

● **Figure 2.2** A summary of the chemical components of an average person.

proteins (18%)

other chemicals 41%

water (59%)

fats (18%)

carbohydrates (0.5%)
other (4.5%)

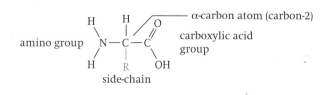

● **Figure 2.3** The general structure of an α-amino acid.

amino group

α-carbon atom (carbon-2)

carboxylic acid group

side-chain

The 20 amino acids differ in the nature of the **R group** that forms the side-chain. These R groups vary in their complexity. In the simplest case the R group is just a hydrogen atom, resulting in the simplest of the amino acids. This is named systematically as 2-aminoethanoic acid, but it is more commonly referred to as glycine. *Figure 2.4* shows the structures of the 20 amino acids used by living organisms.

The 20 different amino acids can usefully be categorised into separate types, according to the nature of the R group. There are three broad categories, depending on whether the R group is non-polar, is polar or can be ionised (containing either acidic or basic groups).

SAQ 2.1

a Name and give the formulae of the two functional groups present in all α–amino acids.

b Which one of the 20 amino acids found in proteins has an unusual structure involving one of these functional groups? What is distinctive about its structure?

c Which α-amino acids have non-polar R groups?

d Which α-amino acids have polar R groups?

e Which two α-amino acids contain acidic groups in their R groups?

The ionisation of amino acids

As you can see in *figure 2.4*, each amino acid contains an acidic group (–COOH) and a basic group (–NH$_2$). As a consequence, these molecules show the properties of both an acid and a base – they are **amphoteric**.

■ In alkaline solution, the acid group can lose a proton (an H$^+$ ion), e.g.:

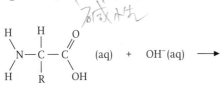

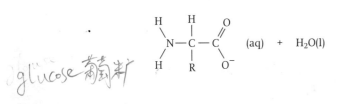

■ In acid solution, the basic amino group can accept a proton, e.g.:

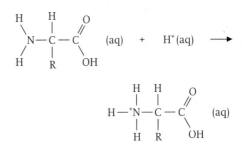

In solution at around pH 7 both the acid and amino groups can be ionised, so amino acids often exist as dipolar ions, known as **zwitterions**.

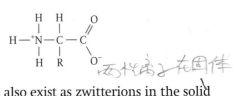

Amino acids also exist as zwitterions in the solid state. Because of this, amino acids show the physical properties characteristic of ionic compounds:

■ they are white solids with melting points (or decomposition points) near 300 °C;

■ they are soluble in water, which is a polar solvent, but largely insoluble in most organic solvents.

The precise charged form of a particular amino acid depends on the pH of the solution. At low pH (high H$^+$ concentration) only the amino groups are charged (–NH$_3^+$). Conversely, at high pH (low H$^+$ concentration) it is only the acid groups that carry a charge (–COO$^-$).

SAQ 2.2

Consider the α-amino acids given in *figure 2.4*.

a (i) What is the R group present in aspartic acid?
   (ii) How will an increase in pH affect the degree of ionisation of the R group of aspartic acid?

b (i) What is the R group present in lysine?
   (ii) How will a decrease in pH affect the degree of ionisation of the R group of lysine?

SAQ 2.3

Lysine contains an amino group in its R group.

a What feature of an amino group means that it can accept a proton (H$^+$ ion) under certain conditions?

b What property does the R group of lysine show as a result of the presence of the amino group?

Non-polar			Polar			Electrically charged		
Name	Abbreviation	Structure	Name	Abbreviation	Structure	Name	Abbreviation	Structure
glycine	Gly		asparagine	Asn		ACIDIC aspartic acid	Asp	
alanine	Ala							
valine	Val		glutamine	Gln		glutamic acid	Glu	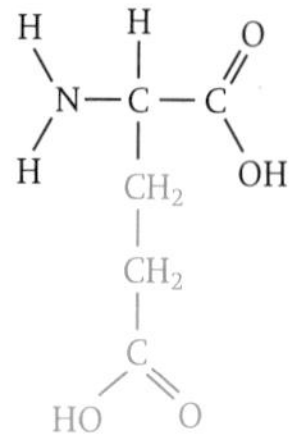
leucine	Leu		tyrosine	Tyr		BASIC arginine	Arg	
isoleucine	Ile		cysteine	Cys				
phenylalanine	Phe		serine	Ser		lysine	Lys	
tryptophan	Trp		threonine	Thr				
proline	Pro					histidine	His	
methionine	Met							

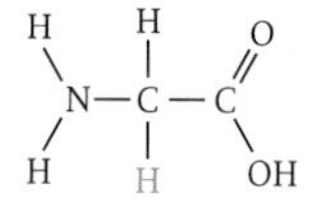

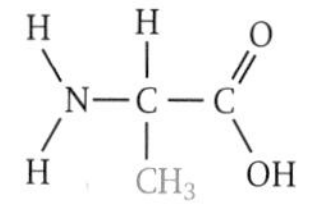

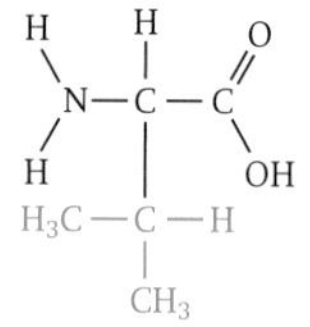

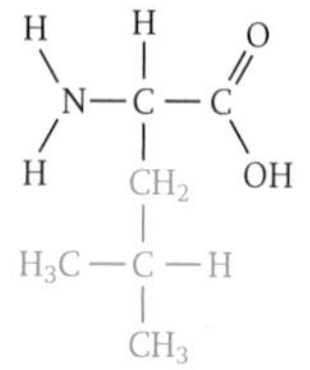

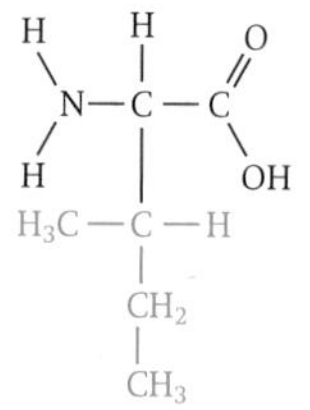

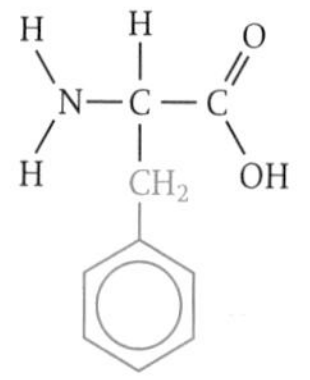

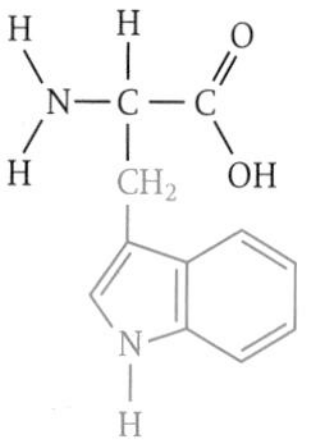

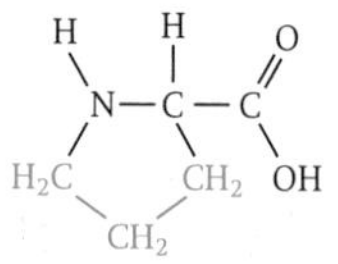

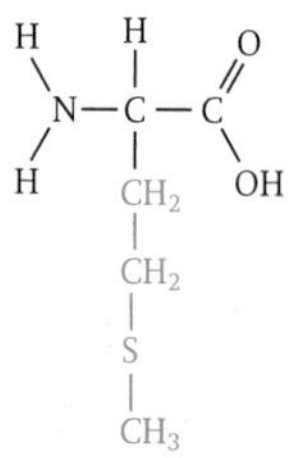

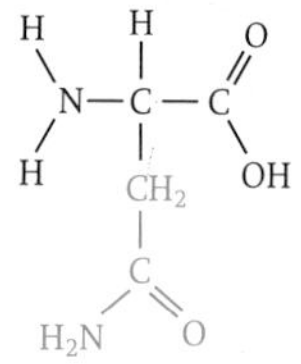

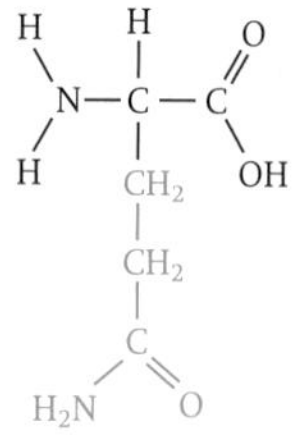

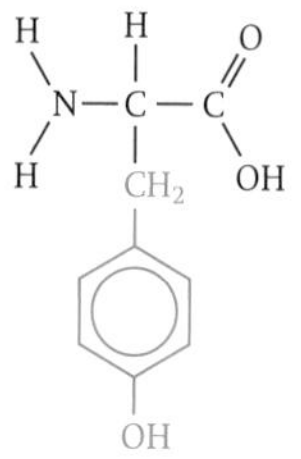

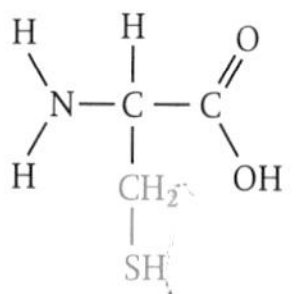

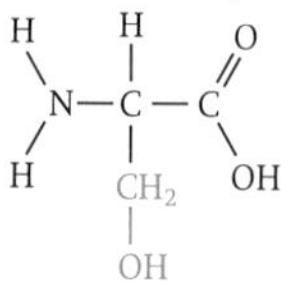

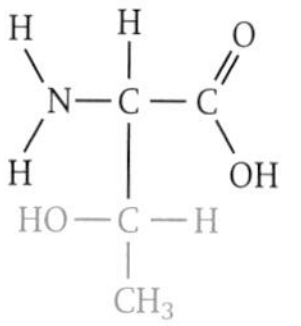

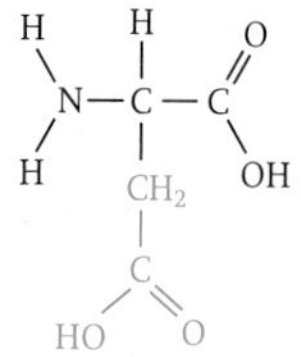

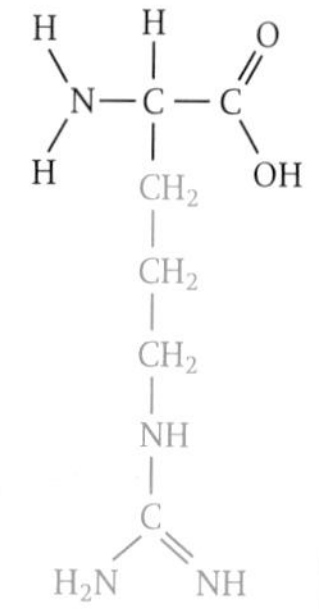

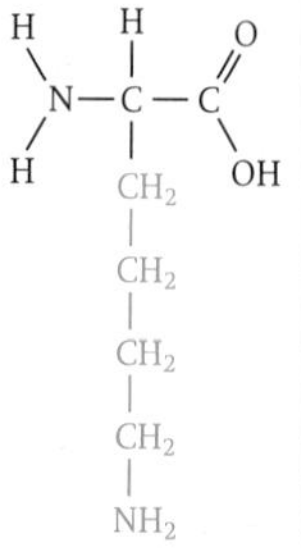

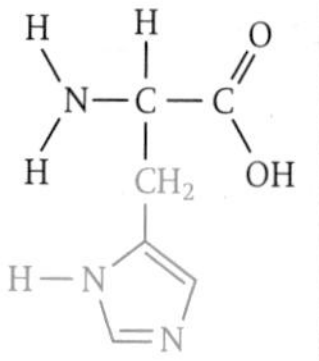

• **Figure 2.4** The structures of the 20 different amino acids found in proteins, grouped in terms of the nature of their R groups. The R groups are drawn in green.

SAQ 2.4

2-Aminocarboxylic acids (α–amino acids) have the general structure shown in *figure 2.3*, where R represents a variety of different side-chains.

a Re-draw this structure, showing the main form in which this general amino acid would exist when in aqueous solution at pH 7.

b What is the overall charge on an amino acid in aqueous solution at pH 7 if R is non-polar?

SAQ 2.5

Alanine is a white crystalline solid that readily dissolves in water. What special features about the structure of the molecule account for:

a its crystalline nature;

b its solubility in water?

Optical isomerism

Molecular shape is tremendously important in biological systems. One example concerns the shape of the amino acids that cells use to build proteins.

So far we have considered amino acids only in a two-dimensional representation. As we have seen, the α-carbon atom in an amino acid is attached to four groups. The *three*-dimensional arrangement around the α-carbon atom is tetrahedral. As an example, the shape of alanine should better be represented as shown in *figure 2.5*.

Note that the α-carbon atom in alanine has four *different* atoms or groups attached to it. As a result, two different isomers of alanine can exist, containing the same groups. These two isomers are mirror image forms of each other which cannot be superimposed on each other (*figure 2.6*). The isomers are known as **optical isomers**, this property is known as **chirality** and the α-carbon atom is known as a **chiral centre** (see *Chemistry 2*, chapter 6). The crucial point here is that biological organisms only use one of these isomeric forms to build proteins (see *Box 2A*, page 12).

SAQ 2.6

a What is the systematic name for glycine?

b Glycine is the only a–amino acid that does not contain a chiral centre. Explain why.

c Which type of stereoisomerism is not shown by glycine but is shown by other a–amino acids?

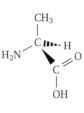

● **Figure 2.5** The tetrahedral structure of alanine. Nitrogen atoms are shown in blue, oxygen atoms in red, carbon atoms in grey and hydrogen atoms in white.

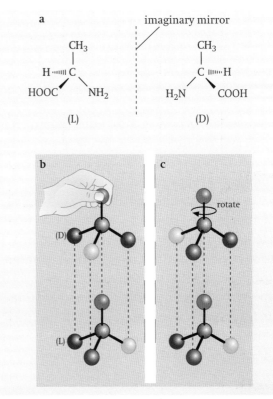

● **Figure 2.6 a** The optical isomers of alanine are mirror images of each other. **b** The two forms are not superimposable on each other – if two groups are in position, the other two are not. **c** If the top model is rotated it cannot be made to fit with the bottom one.

Structure – the key to protein function

So far we have looked at single, isolated amino acids. How are they arrranged or linked to make a protein?

Condensation polymerisation of amino acids

All amino acid molecules contain a carboxylic acid group and an amino group. Therefore, two amino acid molecules can react to form an amide (see *Chemistry 2*, chapter 5). This is known as a

Box 2A The optical activity of amino acid solutions

The isomerism discussed here is a form of stereoisomerism known as optical isomerism. The two optical isomers are given the prefix D- or L- to distinguish them. It is important to note that of the 20 amino acids found in proteins, all but glycine can exist in D and L forms. (Glycine does not show this form of isomerism because its mirror images *can* be superimposed.) However, biological organisms only use the L form to make proteins. A mechanism of protein synthesis involving this built-in stereospecificity exists in all biological organisms (see chapter 6).

The two different stereoisomers of an amino acid are identical in their chemical properties and in the majority of their physical properties – for example their melting points are the same. They can be distinguished by the way they rotate the plane of polarised light.

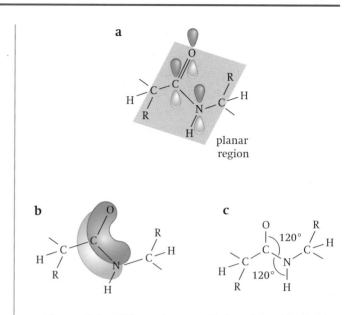

condensation reaction because water is formed in the process. As amino acid molecules each contain two reactive groups, they can act as monomers in the production of a condensation polymer.

For example, glycine and alanine can react to form a **dipeptide** (*figure 2.7*). This dipeptide is an amide made up of two amino acids joined by a **peptide bond** (or amide link). Additional amino acids can react with the dipeptide, firstly to form a tripeptide and then eventually a **polypeptide** chain. In this way a protein can be put together (see chapter 6).

The peptide bond consists of the group

in which the four atoms lie in one plane. Delocalisation of electrons occurs in a π cloud that extends over the O, C and N atoms (see

• **Figure 2.8 a** When the peptide bond (amide link) is formed between two amino acids the link region has a rigid, planar structure. **b** The p orbitals on the carbon and oxygen atoms that form the π bond can also overlap with a p orbital on the nitrogen atom to form a delocalised π orbital over all three atoms. **c** The bond angles are about 120°.

Chemistry 2, chapter 2). This gives the C–N bond some partial double bond character, making free rotation around it impossible. (Compare this with the restriction on free rotation you have come across when considering the C=C group in alkenes.) This restriction means that the peptide bond region has a rigid planar structure with all the bond angles being about 120° (*figure 2.8*).

All proteins are made of one or more unbranched polymer chains formed from many amino acid monomer units. These amino acid units are linked by peptide bonds and the polymers are often referred to as polypeptide chains. A protein is formed when one or more polypeptide chains fold and assemble in a precise and repeatable way to form a three-dimensional structure with biological properties.

The structure of a protein can be considered on three or four levels:

■ primary structure – the sequence of amino acids in a polypeptide chain;

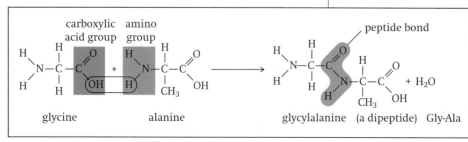

• **Figure 2.7** A condensation reaction between two amino acids produces a dipeptide. The reaction takes place between the carboxylic acid group on one amino acid and the amino group of the other.

- secondary structure – regular structural arrangements of the polypeptide chain that result from hydrogen bonding between peptide bond regions in the chain (see *figure 2.11*);
- tertiary structure – the overall folding of a polypeptide chain that arises from interactions between amino acid side-chains;
- quaternary structure – the manner in which two or more polypeptide chains assemble to form the final protein (not applicable if a protein only has one polypeptide chain).

SAQ 2.7

a What type of polymerisation takes place when a protein chain is assembled from α-amino acids?

b State what you understand by the following terms:
  (i) a tripeptide;
  (ii) a polypeptide;
  (iii) a protein chain.

SAQ 2.8

The diagram below shows the structure of a tetrapeptide at pH 7.

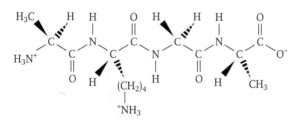

a Copy the structure and draw a ring round a peptide bond on the diagram. Name the functional group involved.

b How many different amino acid residues are linked in the tetrapeptide?

c Complete the drawing of the peptide shown below to show its structure at pH 12.

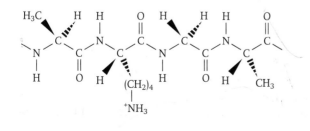

SAQ 2.9

a Draw a diagram showing the bond formed between two amino acids (NH₂CH(R)COOH) during formation of a protein chain. Label the approximate bond angles and describe the shape of the fragment that you have drawn.

b Explain (i) why the structure in this region is rigid, and (ii) why the >C=O group and the >N–H group are arranged *trans* to each other (consider the size of the R groups on each amino acid).

Primary structure

Each polypeptide chain is a linear polymer of amino acids and as such has an amino- (or N-) terminal end and a carboxyl- (or C-) terminal end. The sequence of amino acid **residues** in a chain is known as the **primary structure** of the polypeptide. As an example, the primary structure of the insulin 'A' chain is shown in *figure 2.9* overleaf. (The position in the primary structure of any cysteine residues is of particular significance, as these can form disulphide bridges that stabilise the three-dimensional structure of a protein. See page 16.)

In a cell, polypeptide chains are always synthesised from the N-terminal end to the C-terminal end (see chapter 6). Thus, when writing out the primary sequence of a polypeptide chain the amino acids are numbered from the N-terminal end, as indicated in *figure 2.9*.

Each protein chain is a condensation polymer built from its own unique selection of amino acids. It is not only the mix of amino acids that is unique but also the sequence in which they are joined together along the protein chain. We will see in chapter 6 that this sequence is genetically determined.

SAQ 2.10

a What type of bonding is responsible for maintaining the primary structure of a protein chain?

b A polypeptide chain is said to have direction. How are the two ends of the chain referred to?

Secondary structure

Every polypeptide has a 'backbone' that runs the length of the chain (*figure 2.10*). As the only

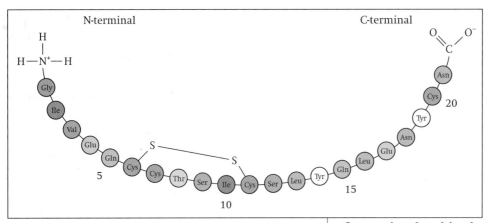

N-terminal   C-terminal

● **Figure 2.9** The primary sequence of the insulin A chain (a short polypeptide of 21 amino acids). Note the cysteine residues at positions 6, 11 and 20 in the chain. They form disulphide bridges (the one between residues 6 and 11 is shown here) that stabilise the three-dimensional structure of the insulin molecule. The abbreviations used are explained in *figure 2.4*.

difference between the amino acids lies in the R groups, this backbone is essentially the same for all proteins (–C–C–N–C–C–N– etc). Although the rigid planar structure of the peptide bond restricts some of the shapes that a polypeptide chain can adopt, the backbone is flexible and in certain sections can fold in a regular manner, known as the **secondary structure**. The folding in the polypeptide backbone is stabilised by hydrogen bonding. The N–H of one peptide bond forms a hydrogen bond to the C=O of another peptide bond (*figure 2.11*).

Two of the most stable types of secondary structure are the α-**helix** and the β-**pleated sheet**. In both these types the polypeptide chain is folded in a very stable arrangement because of the many hydrogen bonds formed between adjacent peptide bond regions.

The α-helix

An α-helix is like a narrow tube. The polypeptide chain is coiled in a spiral, the R groups of the

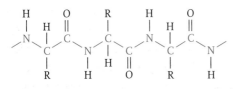

● **Figure 2.10** The backbone of a polypeptide.

amino acid residues project outwards from the spiral, and there are 3.6 residues per turn (*figure 2.12*). Each peptide group is involved in two hydrogen bonds, with the C=O of a peptide group being hydrogen bonded to the N–H of the peptide group four units ahead in the primary structure. The hydrogen bonds run down the length of the α-helix and hold the structure in place.

However, not all amino acids allow such structures to form; some R groups *destabilise* an α-helix. Of particular note here is the amino acid proline.

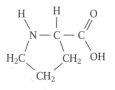

Because of its distinctive cyclic structure, proline breaks up an α-helical region by introducing a sharp kink in the chain.

The β-pleated sheet

In the β-pleated sheet the polypeptide is not coiled, but lengths of the chain lie fully stretched side by side, forming a sheet (*figure 2.13*). The R groups of the amino acid residues point above and below the plane of the sheet while the C=O and N–H groups of the peptide groups in adjacent sections point towards each other. Hydrogen

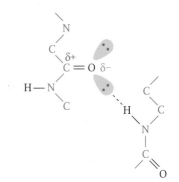

● **Figure 2.11** Hydrogen bonds between peptide bond regions stabilise protein secondary structure.

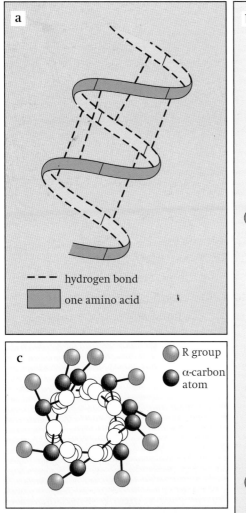

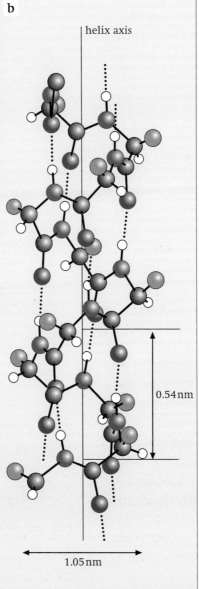

- **Figure 2.12 a** The structure of the α-helix. **b** The helix extends 0.54 nm for each complete turn (this is known as the pitch of the helix). **c** The end-on view shows that the R groups all point outwards from the helix.

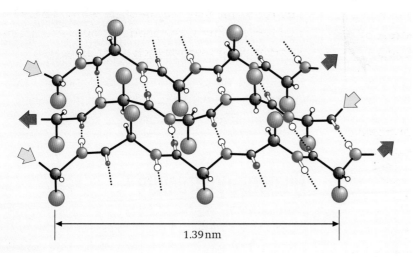

- **Figure 2.13** The β-pleated sheet structure – the R groups point above and below the sheet.

bonds form between these adjacent sections and so stabilise the structure.

SAQ 2.11

a Draw a diagram to show how hydrogen bonds may be formed between two peptide bonds.

b What level of protein structure is involved in the type of hydrogen bond drawn in part **a**?

c Which two major types of structural feature can be created by hydrogen bonding between peptide bond regions?

SAQ 2.12

Linus Pauling won the Nobel Prize for Chemistry in 1954 for establishing the structure of the α-helix in proteins.

a How far does the α-helix extend for each complete turn (this is called the pitch of the helix)?

b How many amino acid units does it take to make one complete turn?

c How far does the α-helix extend for each amino acid unit?

d By how many degrees does the helix twist for each amino acid unit?

Tertiary structure

A series of possible interactions between the R groups of different amino acid residues produces a third level in the hierarchy of protein folding. This is known as the **tertiary structure** and is crucially important to a protein's function.

The three-dimensional shape of a protein chain is maintained by a series of mainly electrostatic interactions between the R groups of the amino acids making the chain. At this level, the chemical nature of the different R groups becomes particularly significant (see *figure 2.4*). The different possible interactions responsible for maintaining the tertiary structure of a polypeptide chain are summarised in *figure 2.14*. These interactions are:

- ionic bonds between charged R groups, such as those of lysine and aspartic acid;
- hydrogen bonds between polar R groups;
- instantaneous dipole-induced dipole forces between non-polar side-chains, such as those of valine and phenylalanine;
- covalent disulphide bonds formed between cysteine residues at different locations in the primary sequence (*figure 2.15*).

The interactions between particular R groups in different regions of a polypeptide chain reinforce a specific folding arrangement. Some of these interactions are relatively easily disrupted, others not so. The formation of disulphide bridges is of particular significance. Because of their covalent nature, disulphide bonds can have the effect of locking a particular tertiary structure in place.

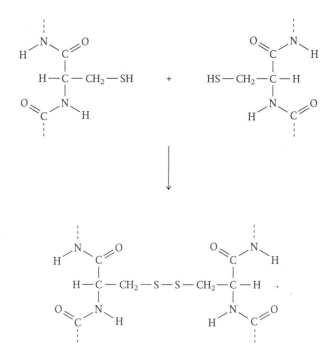

● **Figure 2.15** The formation of a covalent disulphide bond from the R groups of two cysteine residues.

SAQ 2.13
Tertiary structure in proteins is stabilised in part by hydrogen bonds between the R groups of amino acid residues. Consider the R groups present in the amino acids lysine, asparagine, valine and aspartic acid (see *figure 2.4*). For each amino acid, predict whether the R groups can contribute to a hydrogen bond.

SAQ 2.14
Describe how a section of a protein containing valine, glutamic acid and cysteine (see *figure 2.4*) can contribute to the ordered secondary and tertiary structure of a protein with an α-helix. Include diagrams in your answer and discuss the relevant bonds and forces that stabilise the structure.

Quaternary structure

Many proteins consist of two or more polypeptide chains that interact in order to assemble the full protein. The way in which the polypeptide chains are grouped together to form the stable protein molecule is the **quaternary structure** of the

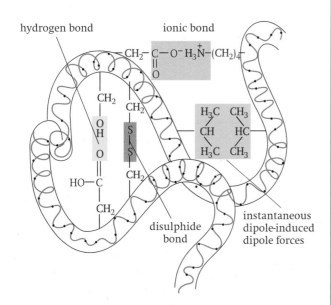

● **Figure 2.14** A summary of the interactions responsible for maintaining the tertiary structure of a polypeptide chain.

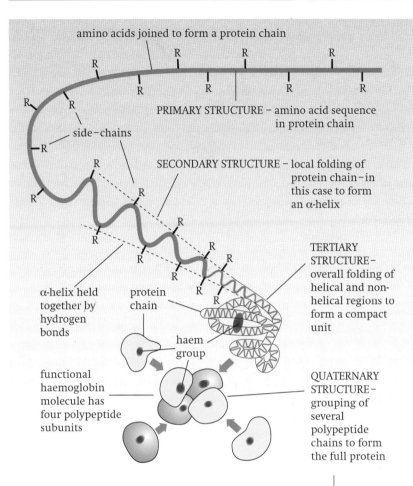

amino acids joined to form a protein chain

PRIMARY STRUCTURE – amino acid sequence in protein chain

side–chains

SECONDARY STRUCTURE – local folding of protein chain – in this case to form an α-helix

α-helix held together by hydrogen bonds

protein chain

haem group

TERTIARY STRUCTURE – overall folding of helical and non-helical regions to form a compact unit

functional haemoglobin molecule has four polypeptide subunits

QUATERNARY STRUCTURE – grouping of several polypeptide chains to form the full protein

• **Figure 2.16** The four different levels of protein structure in haemoglobin.

Haemoglobin – the oxygen carrier

Human **haemoglobin** consists of four protein chains: two identical chains known as α-chains (141 amino acid residues each) and a further two identical chains known as β-chains (146 amino acid residues each). Overall, haemoglobin is described as $\alpha_2\beta_2$. When folded, each chain contains about 70% α-helical secondary structure (*figure 2.17*, overleaf).

Each of the four protein chains is also bound to a non-protein haem group that contains an iron(II) ion (Fe^{2+}). It is the Fe^{2+} ions in the haem groups that bind oxygen to haemoglobin. Each haem group can bind one oxygen molecule and each of the four haem groups binds oxygen simultaneously, so the overall reaction is

$$Hb + 4O_2 \rightleftharpoons HbO_8$$
haemoglobin   oxygen   oxyhaemoglobin

The Fe^{2+} ions act as the centres of complex ions; the ligands are the haem group, the protein chain and a molecule of oxygen (*figure 2.18*, overleaf). The haem group binds to the Fe^{2+} ion via four nitrogen atoms and the protein chain also binds via a nitrogen atom.

protein. The types of forces *between* the chains are the same as those that maintain the tertiary structure of the individual chains.

Figure 2.16 summarises the different levels of protein structure, including quaternary structure, using haemoglobin as an example.

SAQ 2.15 _____

The following table shows the types of interactions or bonds between two amino acid R groups that can stabilise protein tertiary and quaternary structure. Complete the table by filling in spaces **A** to **E**.

Amino acid 1	R group of amino acid 1	R group of amino acid 2	Amino acid 2	Bond/ interaction between R groups
alanine	$-CH_3$	$(CH_3)_2CH-$	valine	A
serine	$-CH_2OH$	NH_2COCH_2-	asparagine	B
aspartic acid	$-CH_2CO_2^-$	$\overset{+}{N}H_3(CH_2)_4-$	lysine	C
cysteine	$-CH_2SH$	$HSCH_2-$	E	D

SAQ 2.16 _____

Haemoglobin is an important protein, which transports oxygen.

a How many different polypeptide chains are there in a haemoglobin molecule?

b (i) Name the non-protein group present in haemoglobin and state how many of these groups are present in each molecule of haemoglobin.

(ii) Which transition metal is part of this non-protein group, and what oxidation state is it in?

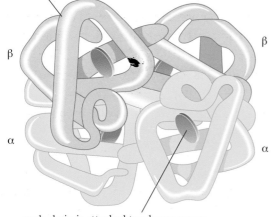

four polypeptide chains make up the haemoglobin molecule – each molecule contains 574 amino acids

β   β

α   α

each chain is attached to a haem group that can combine with oxygen

- **Figure 2.17** The overall structure of haemoglobin. There are two α-chains and two β-chains per molecule. Each chain has an iron-containing haem group associated with it (see also *figure 2.1*, page 7).

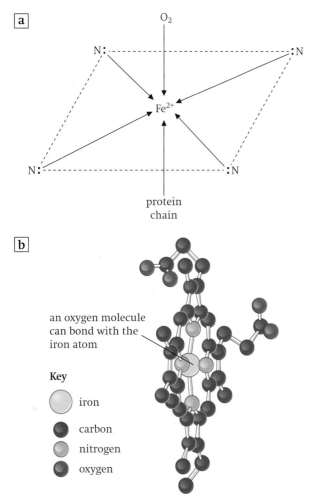

a

O_2

N   N

Fe^{2+}

N   N

protein chain

b

an oxygen molecule can bond with the iron atom

Key

○ iron

● carbon

◐ nitrogen

● oxygen

- **Figure 2.18 a** The complex ion in haemoglobin. **b** The haem group contains an Fe^{2+} ion which can bond reversibly with an oxygen molecule.

The denaturation and hydrolysis of proteins

So far we have studied the formation and structure of proteins. However, it is also important to consider the *disruption* of protein structure, which is known as **denaturation**.

The peptide bonds between the individual amino acids in a polypeptide chain are strong, covalent bonds. However, we have seen that the overall shape and function of a protein depends on weaker interactions that are more easily disrupted. When a protein loses its unique three-dimensional shape it has been **denatured**. This denaturation can be temporary or permanent.

Everyday examples of denaturation include:

- the curdling of milk proteins when milk turns sour or when milk is mixed with vinegar;
- the thermal denaturation of egg or meat protein when it is cooked;
- the mechanical denaturation of egg white when it is whisked (*figure 2.19*).

In all these cases the process is irreversible; the protein cannot be re-assembled.

Proteins may change shape in response to a variety of factors, such as:

- changes in pH;
- changes in temperature;
- disruption of instantaneous dipole-induced dipole forces by certain metal ions, including those of heavy metals;
- the addition of a small polar molecule such as urea ($CO(NH_2)_2$) in concentrated solution – urea causes complete denaturation by specifically disrupting hydrogen bonds;
- the presence of mild reducing agents capable of breaking disulphide bridges.

- **Figure 2.19** Gammon and fried egg, followed by a meringue – a meal of denatured proteins.

Many of the early experiments on protein folding and function were based on studying the effects of urea and reducing agents. Christian Anfinsen won the 1972 Nobel Prize for Chemistry for experiments on the reversible denaturation of an enzyme called ribonuclease.

At a more mundane level, certain types of hair styling involve the breaking and re-making of the disulphide bridges in hair keratin (*figure 2.20*).

Denaturation by altering the pH of a solution

Small changes in pH can alter the ionisation of various R groups without necessarily causing a permanent change in protein conformation. Such changes may affect the activity of an enzyme for example (see chapter 3, page 28). However, more drastic changes in pH (outside the range 3–9) can cause such extensive alteration in the protonation of R groups that the structure of a protein at secondary, tertiary and quaternary levels is destroyed.

For example, the R groups of amino acids such as glutamic acid and lysine are usually charged at around pH 7; they contain a $-COO^-$ and an $-NH_3^+$ group, respectively. As such they could participate in an ionic interaction which might help stabilise a protein structure. At extremes of pH one or other of these groups will lose its charge and so the interaction will be lost. Extensive changes such as this will destabilise protein structure.

● **Figure 2.20** Permed hair is the result of altering the disulphide bonds between adjacent strands of protein in hair.

Denaturation by increasing temperature

Increased temperature gives molecules more energy and consequently disrupts the whole range of weak interactions responsible for maintaining the secondary, tertiary and quaternary structure of proteins. The weakest forces between R groups are the van der Waals' forces between instantaneous dipoles and so these are the first to be broken.

However, if the temperature increase is large enough then most of the forces involved in secondary and tertiary structure are disrupted. The forces involved are not able to maintain the structure against the increased vibrational motion of the polypeptide chains. Irreversible denaturation occurs when secondary and tertiary structure are disrupted to produce random coils. In this condition the chains are so unravelled that they tangle with each other. Temperatures above about 60–70 °C often bring this about.

SAQ 2.17

a Increasing the temperature causes molecules to vibrate more quickly. Explain how this can cause protein denaturation.

b Extremes of pH will cause many of the R groups of the amino acid residues along a polypeptide chain to gain or lose an H^+ ion. Explain how this can break up both secondary and tertiary structure.

Denaturation by metal ions

The presence of certain metal ions can also have a disruptive effect on protein folding by interrupting with Van der Waals' forces. Heavy metal ions (Ag^+ or Hg^{2+}, for example) can also inhibit enzyme activity by reacting with $-SH$ groups in cysteine residues (see chapter 3, page 32).

Complete hydrolysis of proteins

Exposure of protein molecules to heat and concentrated acid results in the complete hydrolysis of the protein chain, that is the breakdown of the primary structure (see *Chemistry 2*, chapter 5). Hydrolysis is the chemical reversal of a condensation reaction. The components of a water molecule (an H atom and an OH group) are added across a covalent bond as the bond is broken.

In the hydrolysis of protein molecules, it is the covalent peptide bonds that are broken. The protein is hydrolysed to give a mixture of its constituent amino acids. The following equation shows the hydrolysis of a tripeptide, alanine-valine-glycine, into its constituent amino acids:

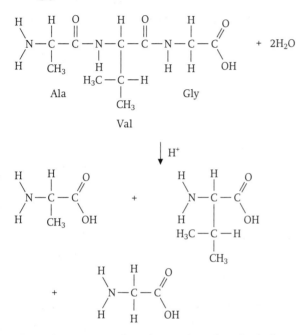

The mixture can then be analysed to find the amino acid composition of the protein. Various chromatographic methods can be used, including paper chromatography (see *box 2B*). This is one of the first steps in working out the structure of a protein. The acid hydrolysis is usually carried out using hydrochloric acid (6 mol dm^{-3}) and refluxing at 100 °C in a sealed tube for 10–24 hours.

Box 2B Analysing amino acid mixtures

One method of identifying amino acids in a mixture is to analyse the sample by paper chromatography. As in all chromatographic methods, there are two phases involved in paper chromatography. In this case the stationary phase is the paper, while the mobile phase is the solvent used.

Samples of pure amino acids and the unknown mixture are spotted onto the paper, which is then dipped in the solvent. The solvent (usually a mixture of butan-1-ol, ethanoic acid and water) moves up the paper carrying the amino acids with it. Those amino acids most soluble in the solvent migrate furthest up the paper. The experiment is stopped just before the solvent reaches the top of the paper. The paper is dried. The amino acids are colourless and to visualise the position of the spots it is necessary to use a locating agent. In this case, ninhydrin is used which reacts with the amino acids to produce purple spots. By measuring the distances moved and comparing with the migration of standard amino acids it is possible to work out the composition of the amino acid mixture.

SAQ 2.18

a A protein that is particularly rich in the amino acid lysine is stable in solution at pH 7. If the pH is increased to 11, the protein is denatured. Give a possible explanation for this observation.

b Suggest why when heavy metal ions such as silver, Ag$^+$, are absorbed by living organisms they have a harmful effect on the activity of enzyme molecules.

SUMMARY

◆ α-Amino acids (2-amino acids) are the biological monomers from which protein molecules are built. There are 20 different amino acids used to make proteins.

◆ α-Amino acids contain both a carboxylic acid group and an amino group, attached to the same carbon atom. They have the general formula $NH_2CH(R)COOH$.

◆ α-Amino acids have different R groups, which can be categorised according to their polar or non-polar nature.

◆ α-Amino acids can act as both an acid and a base and under most circumstances exist in the 'zwitterion' form, $^+NH_3CH(R)COO^-$.

◆ With the exception of glycine, all of the α-amino acids contain a chiral carbon atom and therefore show optical isomerism. Cells always use L-amino acids in protein synthesis.

◆ Proteins are condensation polymers. The amino acid monomers are linked by peptide bonds.

◆ The primary structure of a protein chain is the sequence of amino acids in the chain.

◆ Polypeptide chains have direction, having an amino- (or N-) terminal end and a carboxyl- (or C-) terminal end.

◆ The secondary structure of a protein involves the folding of the polypeptide backbone, stabilised by hydrogen bonding between peptide bond regions of the chains. The two most stable types of secondary structure are the α-helix and the β-pleated sheet.

◆ The tertiary structure of a protein consists of the folding of the polypeptide chain that arises from interactions between the R groups of the amino acid residues. These interactions include instantaneous dipole-induced dipole forces, ionic linkages, hydrogen bonding and covalent disulphide bridges.

◆ The quaternary structure of a protein relates to the manner in which two or more polypeptide chains assemble into the functional protein. The interactions involved are the same as those responsible for tertiary structure.

◆ The functioning of proteins in their biological role is very much linked to their three-dimensional shape.

◆ Haemoglobin is an example of a protein with quaternary structure. Two α-chains and two β-chains assemble to form the oxygen-carrying protein. Oxygen molecules bind to the Fe^{2+} ions in the four haem groups present in the complete protein.

◆ Conditions that interfere with or disrupt the forces that maintain the shape of a protein cause denaturation. Such denaturation can be brought about by heavy metal ions and extremes of pH or temperature.

◆ Treatment of a protein with hot concentrated hydrochloric acid results in hydrolysis of the protein to its constituent amino acids.

Questions

1   Aspartame is an artificial sweetener that is 160 times sweeter than sucrose. It is a dipeptide of the amino acids aspartic acid and phenylalanine, with the methyl ester of phenylalanine forming the C-terminal end. By referring to *figure 2.4*, draw the structure of aspartame.

2   A synthetic polypeptide made from leucine has an average molecular mass of about 3000. The diagram shows part of the polypeptide containing two leucine residues.

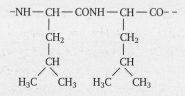

a   Calculate a value for the average number of leucine residues in the polypeptide.

b   (i)   Circle two atoms in the diagram above which might be used to establish the secondary structure of the polypeptide.

(ii)   What kind of intramolecular attraction is available for the maintenance of tertiary structure in the polypeptide?

c   A **different** peptide composed of several amino acids was hydrolysed in aqueous acid. The resulting solution was treated with sodium nitrite which converts primary amino groups, $-NH_2$, to gaseous nitrogen.

$$H_2NCHRCO_2H + NaNO_2 + HCl \rightarrow$$
$$HOCHRCO_2H + H_2O + NaCl + N_2$$

2×10^{-4} mole of peptide gave $28.8\,cm^3$ of nitrogen at room temperature and pressure.

(1.0 mol of nitrogen occupies $24\,dm^3$ at room temperature and pressure).

(i)   How many moles of nitrogen gas were produced?

(ii)   How many amino acid residues does this suggest were linked in 1 molecule of the peptide? Assume that hydrolysis was complete and that the primary amino groups gave a 100% yield of nitrogen.

(iii)   Not all amino acids would give the result found in (ii); name or describe one such amino acid. Explain your answer.

3   a   Electrophoresis is a technique that separates molecules according to their electrical charge. The diagram below shows, in outline, a technique that could be used for separating the amino acids that are obtained when a protein is hydrolysed.

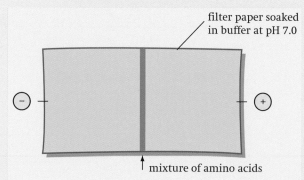

filter paper soaked in buffer at pH 7.0

mixture of amino acids

(i)   After electrophoresis of the amino acid mixture, using the technique shown above, the filter paper is stained with ninhydrin, which gives a purple colour in the presence of amino acids. A small peptide consisting of three amino acid units, shown below, is hydrolysed and the mixture is separated (at pH 7.0), again by electrophoresis.

Copy the diagram of the electrophoresis apparatus and sketch on it the pattern that will be obtained on the filter paper after staining. Explain how you came to your conclusions.

(ii) Explain how the result will be different if the electrophoresis is performed at pH 12.0.

b When a protein chain is folded into its three dimensional structure, it is normally found that amino acids such as valine and isoleucine are found buried in the interior of the protein structure, whereas amino acids such as glutamic acid and lysine are found on the protein surface. By referring to the structures of these amino acids in *figure 2.4*, explain this observation.

4 Hair is made of an insoluble fibrous protein. The shape of hair can be changed in a way that lasts for some time by changing the disulphide (–S–S–) bridges present. Small sulphur-containing molecules such as thioglycollate can bring this about.

Hairdressers first use rollers to create a new style for the hair. They then apply the thioglycollate solution to break apart the disulphide bonds, producing –SH groups. This allows the protein chains to re-arrange themselves to the new shape of the hair. The thioglycollate is thoroughly washed away. The hair is fixed in its new shape (made permanent or 'permed') using a dilute hydrogen peroxide solution which re-forms new disulphide bridges.

a Which insoluble fibrous protein is hair made of?

b Are the disulphide bonds mainly responsible for the secondary, tertiary, or quaternary structure of proteins?

c What types of reaction are (i) the thioglycollate solution, and (ii) the hydrogen peroxide solution carrying out?

d What causes the shaping of the hair to eventually be lost?

CHAPTER 3

Enzymes

By the end of this chapter you should be able to:

1 describe the behaviour of enzymes as *catalysts* of high activity and specificity;

2 explain the concept of the *active site* in enzyme structure;

3 explain the relationship between enzyme and substrate *concentrations* of biochemical systems;

4 distinguish between the different types of inhibition of enzymes: *competitive inhibition* by a similar substrate molecule competing for the active site and *non-competitive inhibition* by heavy metal ions;

5 explain the advantages of *immobilising* enzymes;

6 state the commercial and industrial uses of enzymes, typified by biological washing powders.

Nature's catalysts

Nature can be considered as a chemical industry; it turns out billions of tonnes of a vast range of products every year using the simplest starting materials. The catalysts that make all this possible are enzymes – all large protein molecules. Enzymes take part in the homogeneous catalysis of reactions in an aqueous environment which otherwise would be so slow that life would be impossible. The digestion of food, the release of energy for movement, the copying of genes in reproduction – all of these processes and more rely on enzymes.

Catalysis is discussed generally in *Chemistry 1*, chapter 14. As with inorganic catalysts, enzymes speed up chemical reactions without being used up themselves in the course of the reaction. They provide an alternative reaction pathway that has a lower activation energy barrier than the uncatalysed reaction. Although enzymes function within the rules that define catalytic activity, they differ from inorganic catalysts in several important respects:

■ higher reaction rates – the rates of enzyme-catalysed reactions are typically increased by

factors of 10^6–10^{12} compared to the uncatalysed reaction (*figure 3.1*). These reaction rates are several orders of magnitude greater than those for the corresponding inorganic catalyst (*table 3.1*).

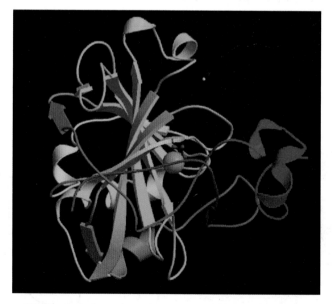

● **Figure 3.1** A computer-generated image of carbonic anhydrase. Carbonic anhydrase catalyses the reaction $CO_2 + H_2O \rightarrow H_2CO_3$ (carbonic acid) within red blood cells and speeds the reaction up by a factor of about one billion. However, if the zinc atom in the centre of the enzyme is removed the enzyme has no activity.

Enzyme	Turnover number
carbonic anhydrase	36 000 000
catalase	5 600 000
β-amylase	1 100 000
β-galactosidase	12 500
phosphoglucose isomerase	1240
succinate dehydrogenase	1150

Turnover number is the number of molecules reacted per enzyme molecule per minute.

● **Table 3.1** Comparison of the catalytic efficiency of certain enzymes.

■ milder conditions – enzyme-catalysed reactions occur under relatively mild conditions: temperatures below 100 °C, atmospheric pressure and usually at pH values around pH 7;

■ greater reaction **specificity** – enzymes are highly selective in their actions; they are usually capable of catalysing the reaction of just one molecule or class of molecules;

■ the reactions are 'clean', with very few side-products;

■ ease of control – the catalytic activities of many enzymes can be varied by altering the concentrations of substances other than the reactant: the way the reaction is controlled can be complex.

Inside a cell, specificity is absolutely essential. For example, an enzyme must be able to distinguish one amino acid from another or recognise a particular sequence of bases in a molecule of DNA. Each enzyme has a specific substrate, the **substrate** being the target molecule acted upon during the enzyme-catalysed reaction.

SAQ 3.1

The table shows the activation energies for the decomposition of hydrogen peroxide under different conditions.

$$2H_2O_2(aq) \rightarrow 2H_2O(l) + O_2(g)$$

Condition	Activation energy $(kJ\,mol^{-1})$
no catalyst	+75.3
platinum catalyst	+48.9
catalase	+23.0

Use the table to decide which condition would give the fastest reaction. Explain your answer.

Box 3A Categorising enzymes

The digestive enzymes of the stomach and small intestine were among the first enzymes to be discovered. These enzymes were given names ending with '-in': hence the names pepsin, trypsin and chymotrypsin. These enzymes are all proteases, meaning that they break proteins down by hydrolysis.

Enzymes are now categorised and named on the basis of six main reaction types (*table 3.2*). As well as ending in '-ase', an enzyme's name also indicates the type of reaction it catalyses and the substrate involved.

What is rather surprising is that there are only six categories of enzyme-catalysed reactions. This illustrates an important point about metabolic systems in cells. The changes achieved by these metabolic pathways are often large, but they are achieved in a series of simple reactions, each catalysed by a specific enzyme. It is the cumulative effect of these small changes that produces the overall large change.

Type of enzyme	Reaction	Example(s)
oxidoreductase	redox reactions, e.g. removal of hydrogen	succinate dehydrogenase, cytochrome oxidase
transferase	transfer of groups, e.g. phosphate group, from one molecule to another	phosphofructokinase, hexokinase
hydrolase	breakdown of molecules by hydrolysis	urease, trypsin, lipase, ribonuclease, amylase
lyase	removal of a group from, or addition to, a double bond	pyruvate decarboxylase
isomerase	isomerisation; moving groups within a molecule	phosphoglucose isomerase, maleate isomerase
ligase	synthetic reactions; joining molecules together	glycogen synthase

● **Table 3.2** The categorisation and naming of enzymes.

Enzyme shape and reactivity

The vast majority of enzymes are water-soluble 'globular' (i.e. curled up in a ball) proteins. The complicated folding of the protein chain to form the tertiary structure gives rise to 'clefts' or 'crevices' of precise geometric shape on the surface of the enzyme. These parts of the enzymes 'recognise' a particular substrate molecule and hold it in place while it reacts – this is possible because this part of the enzyme matches the shape of the substrate. The part of the enzyme where the enzyme-catalysed reaction takes place is known as the **active site** of the enzyme. This region of the enzyme not only 'matches' the shape of the substrate, but contains specific R groups which interact chemically with the substrate. These interactions involve the same forces as are involved in maintaining protein tertiary structure.

The catalytic properties and specificity of an enzyme are determined by the chemical nature of the amino acid R groups at the active site. The active site of an enzyme usually occupies less than 5% of an enzyme's surface area and only involves between 3 and 12 of the amino acids that make up the protein chain of the enzyme. The substrate and active site are complementary structures and the rest of the enzyme structure simply functions as the scaffolding that maintains and protects the shape of the active site.

The 'lock and key' model

In 1894, Emil Fischer proposed a model of enzyme activity that explained the specificity of enzymes. He suggested that substrates bind to enzymes in a similar way to a key fitting into a lock (*figure 3.2*).

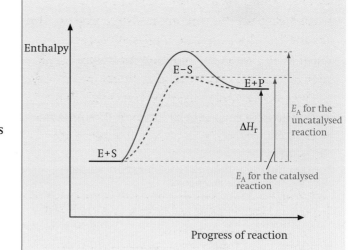

● **Figure 3.3** Energy profile for an enzyme-catalysed endothermic reaction, compared to the same reaction without a catalyst. As for inorganic catalysts, the enzyme provides a different reaction pathway with a lower activation energy (E_A) but the overall enthalpy change (ΔH_r) is unaffected.

Only one substrate will fit the active site, just as only one key fits a lock. This model has become known as the '**lock and key**' model.

The energy profile shown in *figure 3.3* shows how the formation of the **enzyme–substrate complex** reduces the energy requirement for the reaction to proceed. A similar energy profile for an exothermic reaction is shown in *Chemistry 1*, chapter 14.

The overall reaction between the enzyme and its substrate can be represented as:

enzyme + substrate ⇌ enzyme–substrate
(lock)　　(key)　　　　　(key in lock)

The enzyme–substrate complex then undergoes the catalysed reaction:

enzyme–substrate → enzyme + products

The first stage of the reaction is reversible. If the energy available to the enzyme and substrate is less than the activation energy of the reaction, then the enzyme–substrate complex may dissociate without

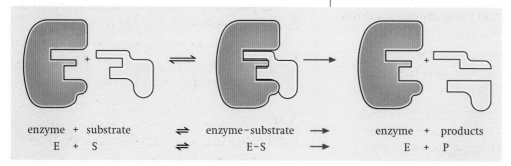

enzyme + substrate ⇌ enzyme–substrate → enzyme + products
　E　+　S　　⇌　　　E–S　　→　　E　+　P

● **Figure 3.2** The 'lock and key' model of enzyme action. The substrate fits precisely into the active site of the enzyme. The enzyme then catalyses the breakdown of the substrate into the products, which can then leave the active site of the enzyme.

product being formed. For some enzymes the second stage of the reaction is also reversible. This makes the whole enzyme-catalysed process capable of proceeding in either direction, depending on the cell's requirements.

Once the products have been formed, they leave the active site of the enzyme. The enzyme is then free to combine with a new substrate molecule.

SAQ 3.2

Explain how the 'lock and key' model describes the mechanism of enzyme action.

SAQ 3.3

a Sketch the energy profile of an uncatalysed exothermic reaction, showing (i) the activation energy (E_A) and (ii) the enthalpy change of reaction (ΔH_r).
b Sketch a similar energy profile for the reaction in part a when the reaction is enzyme-catalysed.

Active site function – substrate binding

The active site of an enzyme has two distinct functions:

■ recognition and binding of the substrate;
■ catalytic action.

In humans, two of the proteases secreted by the pancreas into the small intestine neatly illustrate the subtleties of enzyme activity. Chymotrypsin and trypsin are both enzymes that break down proteins by hydrolysing peptide bonds, but the two enzymes break polypeptide chains in different places:

■ chymotrypsin hydrolyses the peptide bond immediately after a non-polar aromatic amino acid (phenylalanine, for example);
■ trypsin hydrolyses the peptide bond immediately after a basic residue (arginine, for example).

The substrate-binding regions of the two active sites must be different. That of chymotrypsin must consist of non-polar R groups that will be able to interact with aromatic amino acids, whereas that of trypsin will need to involve acidic R groups.

Active site function – catalytic action

The conversion of substrates into products at an active site is carried out by specific R groups. It is important to note that when looking at the primary structure of an enzyme, these R groups are often found to be very far apart in the polypeptide chain. For example, the three R groups involved in the catalytic action of chymotrypsin are those of histidine (residue 57), aspartic acid (residue 102) and serine (residue 195). It is the folding involved in the tertiary structure of the enzyme that brings these groups into position to carry out their catalytic function. This is why conditions which alter protein folding can have such significant effects on the activity of enzymes (see chapter 2, page 19).

The three R groups involved in the active site of chymotrypsin act together by transferring protons (H^+ ions) between themselves. They act in such a way as to leave the R group of serine with an ionised $-O^-$ group.

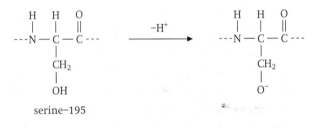

serine–195

This is something that would not normally happen in aqueous solution at the weakly alkaline pH of the small intestine. The negatively charged serine residue attacks the substrate as a nucleophile, bringing about the hydrolysis of a peptide bond. (Nucleophilic reactions are discussed in *Chemistry 1*, chapter 12, and *Chemistry 2*, chapter 3.)

This particular example illustrates a feature of enzyme catalysis. An active site is a micro-environment in which the properties of chemical groups are altered so they can take part in reactions that would not occur in free aqueous solution.

SAQ 3.4

a What two functions does the active site of an enzyme play in the catalysis of a chemical reaction?
b Explain why the roles of enzymes in biological reactions are specific to only one reaction.

Factors affecting enzyme activity

Enzyme activity is highly dependent on the three-dimensional tertiary structure of the enzyme molecule (see chapter 2, page 15) and hence on the relatively weak interactions that control the tertiary structure. These weak interactions are also involved in the binding of the substrate to the active site of the enzyme. Recognition between the substrate and the active site and molecular 'fit' are the key ideas behind enzyme activity. Even subtle changes in temperature or pH can modify the interactions involved, resulting in an enzyme working at less than maximum efficiency.

As with any homogeneous catalyst (see *Chemistry 1*, chapter 14, and *Chemistry 2*, chapter 12), the rate of an enzyme-controlled reaction is affected by the concentration of the substrate and the concentration of the enzyme itself. Interactions with other molecules, either at the active site or elsewhere on the protein surface, can result in control or inhibition of enzyme activity.

The effect of temperature

The effect of temperature on enzyme activity is complex because it is the outcome of several different factors. These are:
- the speed of the molecules;
- the activation energy of the catalysed reaction;
- the thermal stability of the enzyme and the substrate.

At relatively low temperatures (around 0 °C), the rate of most enzyme-catalysed reactions is very low because the molecules involved in the reaction:
- have low speeds and so do not collide frequently;
- do not possess the activation energy required for reaction to occur (see *Chemistry 1*, chapter 14).

The invention of refrigeration revolutionised food storage and transport precisely because enzyme-catalysed reactions are slowed down at low temperatures.

Between 0 °C and approximately 40 °C, the rate of enzyme activity increases almost linearly, approximately doubling every 10 °C, because:
- the molecules involved move faster and so collide more frequently;

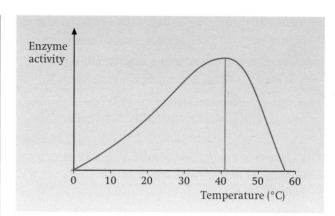

● **Figure 3.4** How the activity of a typical enzyme alters with temperature.

- a greater proportion of the collisions involve molecules with an energy greater than the activation energy for the catalysed reaction.

For most enzymes the rate of reaction starts to decrease above 40 °C. This is because the enzyme molecules are progressively denatured (see chapter 2, page 19), causing the shape of the active site to change. Above 65 °C, the enzymes from most organisms are completely denatured.

Figure 3.4 summarises the way enzyme activity alters with temperature.

However, there are organisms that show adaptation to the high temperatures of hot springs and deep-sea thermal vents (see *figure 1.3*). Enzymes from these organisms retain activity at 80 °C or higher. These enzymes provide fascinating models for studying the modifications of protein structure necessary to maintain enzyme function at high temperatures.

The effect of pH changes

Enzyme activity is dependent upon pH (see chapter 2, page 19):
- Extremes of pH (high acidity or high alkalinity) will denature proteins by disrupting the precise three-dimensional arrangement of the protein chains.
- Small changes in pH can affect the ionisation of the substrate and/or the ionisation of the R groups of the amino acids in the active site, reducing the activity of the enzyme (*figure 3.5*).

For example, if the activity of an enzyme depends on some R groups in the active site being charged, then a shift of just one pH unit can change the enzyme activity significantly. Most enzymes are

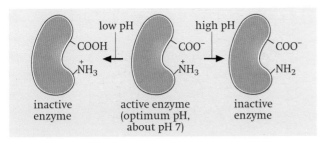

- **Figure 3.5** A change in pH can alter the ionisation of R groups involved in the active site of an enzyme.

active over a fairly narrow range of pH and each enzyme has its own distinct optimum pH.

Digestive enzymes show this clearly (*figure 3.6*).

- Pepsin hydrolyses proteins to peptides in the very acidic conditions of the stomach.
- Amylase, found in saliva, hydrolyses starch to a mixture of glucose and maltose. Saliva is approximately neutral.
- Trypsin hydrolyses peptides to amino acids in the mildly alkaline conditions of the small intestine.

SAQ 3.5

a Sketch a graph to show how the activity of an enzyme varies with temperature.

b Sketch a graph to show how the activity of an enzyme depends on the pH of the medium in which it operates.

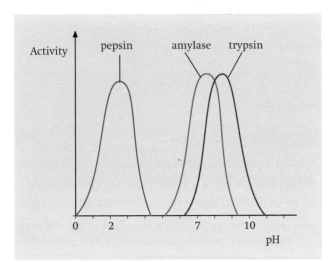

- **Figure 3.6** The pH profiles for pepsin, amylase and trypsin. Pepsin is a protease present in the stomach (acid conditions), amylase is found in saliva (almost neutral conditions) and hydrolyses starch, while trypsin hydrolyses proteins in the alkaline conditions of the small intestine.

SAQ 3.6

The turnover number of an enzyme is the number of substrate molecules that one molecule of an enzyme can convert to product in one minute under optimum conditions.

The turnover numbers of several enzymes are given in *table 3.1*.

a In measuring the turnover number of a particular enzyme, there must be an excess of the substrate present. Why is this so?

b (i) What effect would a fall in temperature of 10 °C have on the turnover number of the enzymes?

   (ii) Explain your answer.

Concentration effects

The concentrations of both enzyme and substrate affect the rate of an enzyme-catalysed reaction. If a fixed amount of enzyme is added to an excess of substrate, the amount of product formed can be followed during the reaction. A progress curve for the reaction is obtained (*figure 3.7*). This is a curve rather than a straight line because the substrate concentration falls as the enzyme catalyses the reaction.

The rate of reaction is fastest at the start of the reaction; this is known as the initial rate of reaction. If the reaction is carried out at various different enzyme concentrations and the initial

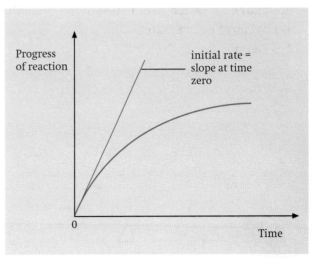

- **Figure 3.7** A curve showing the progress of an enzyme-catalysed reaction. The initial rate of the reaction can be found by drawing a tangent to the curve at time = 0.

rate measured in each case, a plot of initial rate against enzyme concentration can be made (*figure 3.8*). This graph is a straight line, showing that the rate of reaction is directly proportional to enzyme concentration; the reaction is first order with respect to enzyme concentration (see *Chemistry 2*, chapter 12, for more information on orders of reaction).

The effect of substrate concentration on reaction rate can be studied in similar experiments. In this case, initial rates are measured using the same concentration of enzyme and different substrate concentrations (*figure 3.9*). One would expect the rate of reaction to be proportional to the substrate concentration. This is indeed true for relatively low substrate concentrations – the reaction is first order with respect to substrate concentration.

At high substrate concentrations the graph of reaction rate against substrate concentration flattens out, reaching a maximum value (V_{max}). Under these conditions, the reaction is zero order with respect to substrate concentration. This means that at high substrate concentrations it is possible to **saturate** the enzyme molecules with substrate. If all the active sites of the enzyme molecules are occupied, then adding more substrate molecules cannot affect the rate of reaction. Under these conditions, the rate of reaction depends on the rate at which the products leave the active site.

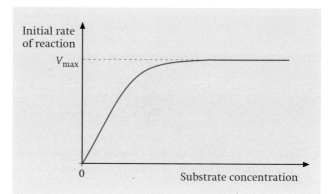

● **Figure 3.9** A graph showing the initial rate of an enzyme-catalysed reaction plotted against substrate concentration. At low substrate concentrations the straight line shows that enzyme activity is proportional to substrate concentration. At high substrate concentrations the rate reaches a maximum (V_{max}).

Inhibition of enzyme activity

An **inhibitor** is a chemical other than the substrate, whose presence affects enzyme function. Some inhibitors, including many toxins, totally inactivate the enzyme; their effects are irreversible. Examples are the organophosphate nerve gases, such as sarin, which inactivate enzymes involved in nerve conduction. Less drastic, reversible, inhibition of enzyme activity is also possible. Indeed, reversible inhibition is an important mechanism for controlling enzyme activity in metabolic 'pathways' (sequences of chemical reactions in the cell, linked in complex series to achieve key processes in many small steps).

Enzyme inhibition can also be competitive or non-competitive.

Competitive inhibition

Competitive inhibitors of a particular enzyme are molecules that have a similar shape and similar chemical characteristics to the substrate molecule. Such molecules can bind to the active site but then cannot participate in the catalysed reaction. When competitive inhibitors are present in the active site no catalysis can take place since the correct substrate cannot attach to the enzyme. When such an inhibitor is added to an enzyme–substrate mixture there is competition between the substrate and the inhibitor to occupy

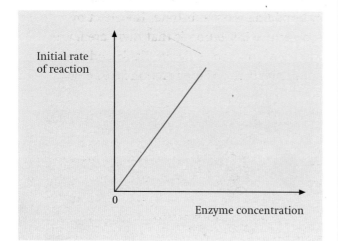

● **Figure 3.8** A graph showing the initial rate of an enzyme-catalysed reaction plotted against enzyme concentration. The straight line shows that enzyme activity is directly proportional to enzyme concentration.

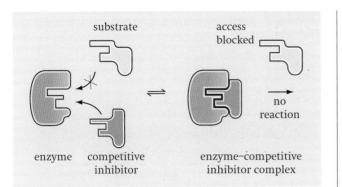

● **Figure 3.10** A model of competitive inhibition. The competitive inhibitor has a very similar shape to the substrate and binds to the active site. However, it does not undergo the catalysed reaction and blocks the enzyme molecule from binding to the substrate.

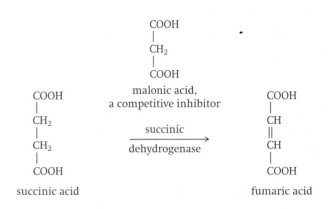

● **Figure 3.12** The enzyme succinic dehydrogenase is competitively inhibited by malonic acid. Malonic acid is very similar in shape to the substrate, succinic acid.

the active sites on the enzyme molecules. The result of this competition depends on the relative concentrations of the substrate and inhibitor.

Competitive inhibition is reversible since the inhibitor does not bind permanently to the active site – the active site is merely temporarily blocked (*figure 3.10*). The maximum rate of reaction (V_{max}, see *figure 3.9*) is the same both with or without the competitive inhibitor, but when the inhibitor is present a much higher substrate concentration is needed to achieve the maximum rate (*figure 3.11*).

An example of competitive inhibition is the inhibition of the enzyme succinate dehydrogenase by molecules such as malonic acid which structurally resemble the substrate, succinic acid (*figure 3.12*).

Non-competitive inhibition

In **non-competitive inhibition**, the inhibitor binds to the enzyme and prevents the catalysed reaction from occurring. However, the inhibitor does not bind to the enzyme's active site. Instead it binds to another part of the enzyme structure. This binding is thought to cause one of the following:

■ the active site to change shape so that the substrate cannot bind (*figure 3.13*);
■ the enzyme–substrate complex to change shape so that catalysis cannot take place.

In non-competitive inhibition, the inhibitor is not shaped like the substrate and there is no competition between the substrate and the inhibitor. The inhibition cannot be overcome simply by adding more substrate. The effect of non-competitive inhibition is that there are fewer functional enzyme molecules available and so the maximum rate (V_{max}) of the reaction is lowered

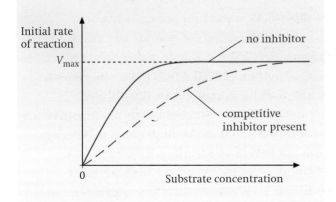

● **Figure 3.11** The effect of a competitive inhibitor on the rate of an enzyme-catalysed reaction. The rate of reaction can reach V_{max}, but only at a higher concentration of substrate.

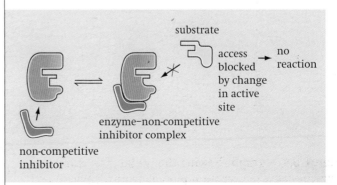

● **Figure 3.13** Non-competitive inhibition: the inhibitor binds to the enzyme and distorts its shape so that it cannot function.

(*figure 3.14*). This reduction in V_{max} can be used to distinguish non-competitive inhibition from competitive inhibition.

As with competitive inhibition, most non-competitive inhibitors only bind weakly to the enzyme. If the concentration of inhibitor falls, the enzyme–inhibitor complex dissociates and the functional shape of the enzyme is restored. Therefore the inhibition is reversible.

One example of non-competitive inhibition involves the effect of heavy metal ions (for example, silver, Ag^+, or mercury, Hg^{2+}) on enzymes with amino acid residues that contain –SH groups. The heavy metal ions react reversibly with these groups, replacing the hydrogen atom with a heavy metal atom.

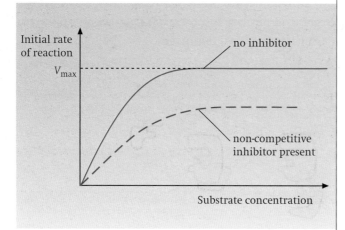

The resulting change in the enzyme disrupts the structure of the enzyme enough to prevent the catalysed reaction taking place. The enzyme is temporarily denatured (see page 19).

● **Figure 3.14** The effect of a non-competitive inhibitor on the rate of an enzyme-catalysed reaction. V_{max} for the inhibited reaction is lower because the inhibitor reduces the concentration of functional enzyme molecules.

SAQ 3.7

The addition of a phosphate group to glucose is the first step in the breakdown of glucose and is universally catalysed by an enzyme called hexokinase.

a   (i)   Sketch a graph to show how the rate of this reaction changes as a fixed amount of the enzyme is reacted with increasing concentrations of glucose (label the line **S**).
   (ii) Explain the shape of your graph.
b   Some compounds can inhibit the rate of an enzyme-catalysed reaction.
   (i)   On your graph from part **a**(i), draw a second line to show the effect of a competitive inhibitor (label this line **C**).
   (ii) Explain how a competitive inhibitor functions.
c   (i)   On your graph from part **a**(i), draw a third line to show the effect of a non-competitive inhibitor (label this line **N**).
   (ii) Explain how a non-competitive inhibitor functions.

Industrial and commercial uses of enzymes

Enzymes are of great commercial and industrial importance because of their enormous catalytic power in aqueous solution at normal temperatures and pressures. *Table 3.3* shows the advantages that biological production systems (generally called **biotechnology**) have over non-biological chemical processes.

The world market for enzymes is worth hundreds of millions of pounds. For example, Novozymes, a world leader in enzyme production, manufactures 75 different types of enzyme and markets them in more than 120 different countries. The largest uses are in the manufacture of detergents and in the food industry. There are also increasing applications in the areas of medical research, diagnosis and treatment.

Research on enzymes has been carried out only relatively recently. Despite this, the production of many foods, such as bread and cheese, and alcoholic drinks, such as wine and beer, has always involved the use of enzymes. These

Box 3B Feedback control by non-competitive inhibition

Feedback control by reversible non-competitive inhibition plays an important role in the delicate control of biochemical processes. This occurs when the end-product of a metabolic pathway inhibits an enzyme early in the pathway and so lowers the activity of the enzyme. This prevents too much of the end-product being formed.

When demand for the end-product increases, its concentration falls. The end-product molecules no longer inhibit the enzyme and activity is restored. This enables metabolic processes to respond quickly to immediate demands. Feedback control is summarised in *figure 3.15*.

A simple example of feedback control can be seen in the use of a thermostat to control the temperature of a room. Here the end-product is the heat produced by a radiator. When more heat is needed (as, for example, when cold air comes in through an open door), then the thermostat switches the radiator on. When the room is hot enough and no more heat is needed, the thermostat switches the radiator off.

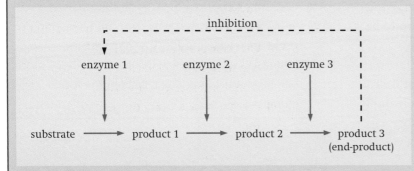

- **Figure 3.15** Feedback control. If the concentration of the end-product becomes too high, then it may act as a non-competitive inhibitor of enzyme 1. The rate of reaction of the whole sequence is controlled by the concentration of the end-product.

traditional uses of enzymes involve intact micro-organisms (yeast and bacteria) and have the advantage that all the necessary reactants are present within the micro-organisms. Perfect conditions for enzyme activity can be produced relatively easily.

Immobilised enzymes

A newer industry of enzyme technology, using enzymes that have been extracted and purified from organisms, now has many commercial applications. Enzymes are catalysts, and so remain unaltered by the reaction process; as a result, it should be possible to re-use them. However, it is often difficult to remove enzymes from the reaction mixture because they are soluble in water. This problem has been overcome by the development of **immobilised enzymes**.

Factor	Chemical/non-biological processing	Biological processing
temperature	very high or low temperatures often required to make the reaction occur – low temperatures are sometimes required to maintain stability of the catalyst or ensure solvents do not boil	moderate temperatures usually employed – heating or refrigeration costs are lower
solvent	organic solvents often needed – may be both expensive and toxic	water is the normal solvent for the enzymic reaction mixture or the growth medium
catalyst	inorganic catalysts often used – often toxic, expensive and lacking in specificity – unwanted by-products may be produced	enzymes are highly specific, therefore less wasteful of substrate and fewer by-products formed
conditions	extremely acidic or alkaline conditions often used – requires expensive corrosion-resistant vessels	moderate pH usually used
cost	raw materials often expensive	raw material usually inexpensive
length of reaction	lengthy preparation time often required	short fermentation or reaction times employed – higher production rate

- **Table 3.3** The advantages of enzyme biotechnology.

For prolonged use in industrial processes, an enzyme can be immobilised by attachment to a solid surface. The overall advantages of this technology are that:

- the enzyme can be easily removed from a reaction mixture by centrifuging or filtration;
- the enzyme can be packed into columns and used continuously for long periods;
- the products can be easily removed from the reaction mixture so that inhibition of the reaction by the end-product can be avoided;
- the stability of the enzyme to thermal denaturation can be increased, enabling the enzyme to be used for longer periods;
- the optimum temperature of the enzyme may be increased, also allowing the reaction to be carried out at higher temperatures, so increasing the rate of reaction.

The initial costs of preparing the immobilised enzyme may be significantly greater than simply using the free enzyme. However, the ability to use the enzyme for longer under more productive conditions makes the use of the immobilised enzyme more economic overall.

The industrial importance of this idea has led to several different methods of immobilisation being explored. The enzyme can be bound to a solid support either by weak intermolecular forces or by covalent bonding. The various methods of immobilisation currently in use are summarised in *figure 3.16*:

- adsorption onto an insoluble matrix;
- covalent binding onto a solid support;
- entrapment within a gel;
- encapsulation behind a selectively permeable membrane.

Each of the methods shown in *figure 3.16* has been successfully used in a variety of applications. The key to success is that the interaction with the support must not interfere with the shape of the active site.

For example, the production of high fructose syrup, which is used as a sweetener in the food industry, requires the conversion of glucose into fructose. Glucose, from the hydrolysis of starch, is converted into the much sweeter compound fructose using the enzyme glucose isomerase. This enzyme has proved easy to immobilise and can be used in a continuous reactor at 60–65 °C and pH 7 for over 1000 hours. The use of immobilised enzyme has dramatically reduced the cost of producing high fructose syrup.

SAQ 3.8

a What is an immobilised enzyme?

b Briefly describe two ways in which enzymes can be immobilised.

c What economic and technical advantages are there to using immobilised enzymes?

d Give an example of the use of immobilised enzymes and explain why they are chosen in preference to using the 'free' enzyme.

e Suggest three reasons why enzymes are of more benefit than chemical catalysts in the food industry.

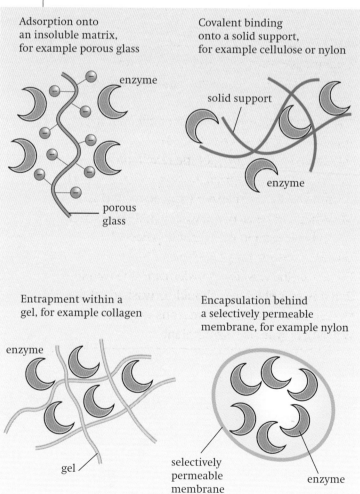

Adsorption onto an insoluble matrix, for example porous glass

enzyme

porous glass

Covalent binding onto a solid support, for example cellulose or nylon

solid support

enzyme

Entrapment within a gel, for example collagen

enzyme

gel

Encapsulation behind a selectively permeable membrane, for example nylon

selectively permeable membrane

enzyme

● **Figure 3.16** Methods of enzyme immobilisation.

Enzymes in washing powders

'Biological' washing powders are those that contain enzymes (*figure 3.17*). The first biological washing powders to be produced contained a protease called subtilisin. (Proteases are enzymes that break down proteins.) Subtilisin removed protein stains such as blood and egg, was stable at the alkaline pH of the detergent and retained its activity at temperatures of up to 60 °C. Subtilisin has since been adapted to be effective at different temperatures. Different forms of subtilisin are added to washing powders depending on whether they are to be used in washes at 40 °C, 50 °C or 60 °C.

Modern biological washing powders are also likely to contain an amylase to digest starch-based stains and a lipase to digest fat-based stains. The most recent powders also contain a cellulase (an enzyme that breaks down cellulose) to 'condition' the fabric. The cellulase enzyme removes stray ends of fibres produced by wear on the fabric.

● **Figure 3.17** Biological washing powders.

SAQ 3.9

A commercial washing powder contains two enzymes. Laboratory tests show that amylase is not present.

a The washing powder contains a buffer so that a solution in water has a pH of 10.8.
   (i) Explain the meaning of the term *buffer*.
   (ii) Show, with a diagram, how you would expect the activity of an enzyme to vary with pH.

b (i) What two types of enzyme would you expect to be present in the washing powder?
   (ii) Give reasons for your choices.

c Packets of the washing powder carry the warning that it is an irritant and should be washed off the skin at once. Suggest two reasons why the washing powder is a skin irritant.

SUMMARY

◆ Enzymes are biological catalysts – they speed up chemical reactions without being altered by the overall reaction. They achieve their effect by providing an alternative reaction pathway that has a lower activation energy than the uncatalysed reaction.

◆ Enzymes are proteins and are able to catalyse in aqueous solutions under mild conditions of temperature and pH. They show a high degree of specificity – generally catalysing only one particular reaction – and are remarkably efficient.

◆ Each enzyme has a specific substrate – the target molecule, or class of molecules, acted upon during the catalysed reaction.

◆ The function of an enzyme depends on its three-dimensional shape – in particular the precise shape of the active site. This region of the enzyme's surface is designed to recognize the particular substrate of the enzyme.

◆ Enzyme–substrate recognition is often referred to as a 'lock-and-key' mechanism. The active site of an enzyme has two functions: it is a binding site for the substrate and a catalytic site which completes the enzyme-catalysed reaction.

◆ Enzyme-catalysed reaction are particularly sensitive to conditions of temperature and pH. They show characteristic temperature and pH optima.

◆ When initial reaction rate is plotted against substrate concentration a plateau is reached at which all the active sites of the enzyme molecules are occupied – no more substrate molecules can attach to the enzyme until some are detached. This maximum reaction rate for a given concentration of enzyme is referred to as V_{max}.

◆ There are two common types of reversible inhibition of enzymes, competitive and non-competitive inhibition. In competitive inhibition the inhibitor has a similar shape to the substrate and competes with the substrate to bind to the active site. In non-competitive inhibition the inhibitor does not bind to the active site but elsewhere on the enzyme. This binding alters the shape of the enzyme sufficiently to prevent the catalysed reaction from taking place.

◆ Isolated enzymes are now used commercially. The effectiveness of enzymes in this context is increased if the enzyme is immobilised. Immobilised enzymes can be easily removed from a reaction mixture and feedback inhibition by reaction products can be avoided. Immobilisation can also improve the thermal stability of an enzyme.

◆ Enzymes are used widely in washing powders to destroy organic material in stains and to condition fabrics. The enzymes are chosen specifically for their activity at different temperatures.

Questions

1 Catalase is an enzyme that catalyses the decomposition of hydrogen peroxide.

$$2H_2O_2(aq) \rightarrow 2H_2O(l) + O_2(g)$$

The graph below shows how the decomposition of hydrogen peroxide varies with the concentration of hydrogen peroxide in the reaction mixture, assuming that the enzyme concentration and temperature are kept constant.

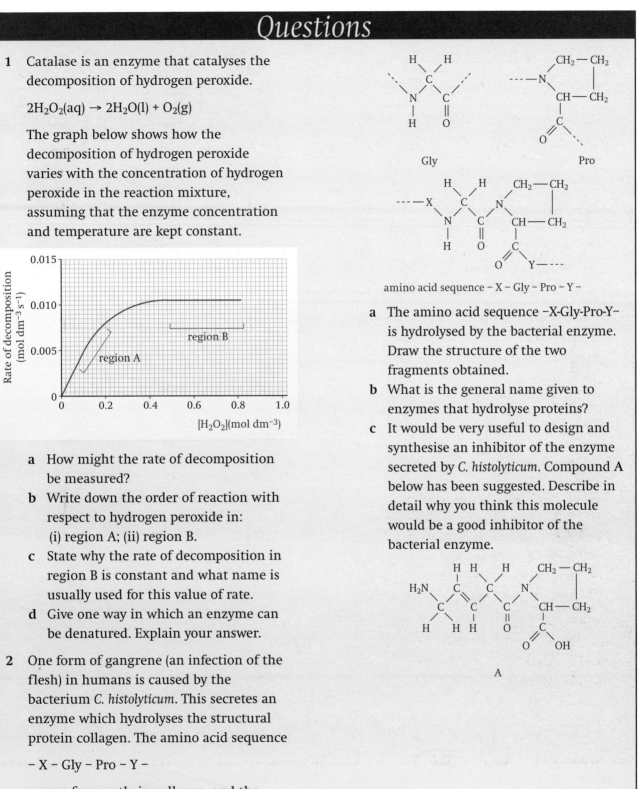

amino acid sequence – X – Gly – Pro – Y –

a How might the rate of decomposition be measured?

b Write down the order of reaction with respect to hydrogen peroxide in:
(i) region A; (ii) region B.

c State why the rate of decomposition in region B is constant and what name is usually used for this value of rate.

d Give one way in which an enzyme can be denatured. Explain your answer.

2 One form of gangrene (an infection of the flesh) in humans is caused by the bacterium *C. histolyticum*. This secretes an enzyme which hydrolyses the structural protein collagen. The amino acid sequence

– X – Gly – Pro – Y –

occurs frequently in collagen, and the bacterial enzyme always hydrolyses this sequence between X and Gly. Gly and Pro are the amino acid residues derived from glycine and proline respectively. X and Y can be any amino acid residues forming part of the protein structure.

a The amino acid sequence –X-Gly-Pro-Y– is hydrolysed by the bacterial enzyme. Draw the structure of the two fragments obtained.

b What is the general name given to enzymes that hydrolyse proteins?

c It would be very useful to design and synthesise an inhibitor of the enzyme secreted by *C. histolyticum*. Compound A below has been suggested. Describe in detail why you think this molecule would be a good inhibitor of the bacterial enzyme.

3   The structure of a tyrosine residue in a polypeptide, at pH 7.0, is shown:

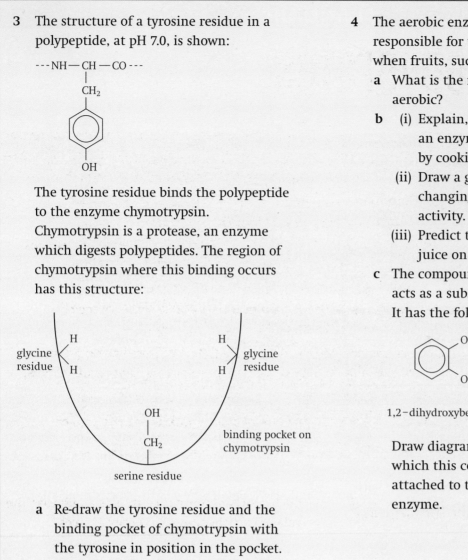

The tyrosine residue binds the polypeptide to the enzyme chymotrypsin.
Chymotrypsin is a protease, an enzyme which digests polypeptides. The region of chymotrypsin where this binding occurs has this structure:

a   Re-draw the tyrosine residue and the binding pocket of chymotrypsin with the tyrosine in position in the pocket. State the two kinds of intermolecular attraction involved.
b   (i) What is the function of a protease?
    (ii) Why are proteases often included in biological washing powders?

4   The aerobic enzyme polyphenol oxidase is responsible for the browning reaction when fruits, such as apples, are cut.
a   What is the meaning of the term aerobic?
b   (i)   Explain, in terms of structure, why an enzyme's activity is decreased by cooking.
    (ii) Draw a graph showing the effect of changing pH on an enzyme's activity.
    (iii) Predict the effect, if any, of lemon juice on the activity of the enzyme.
c   The compound 1,2-dihydroxybenzene acts as a substrate for the enzyme. It has the following structure:

1,2–dihydroxybenzene

Draw diagrams to show two ways in which this compound might be attached to the active site of the enzyme.

CHAPTER 4

Carbohydrates

By the end of this chapter you should be able to:

1 describe the *open-chain structure* of a pentose (for example ribose) and a hexose (for example glucose);

2 describe the α- and β-pyranose *ring structures* of D-glucose;

3 describe the structure of a disaccharide, including the nature of the *glycosidic link* in maltose and cellobiose;

4 describe the structure of polysaccharides, for example cellulose and starch (amylose and amylopectin), as *condensation polymers* and in terms of their glycosidic links (to include 1α-4, 1β-4 and 1α-6 links);

5 suggest how the structures and properties of cellulose, starch and glycogen make them suitable for their role as *structural or storage polymers* in plants and animals;

6 describe the enzyme hydrolysis and acid hydrolysis of the glycosidic linkage;

7 compare the solubilities of monosaccharides and polysaccharides in terms of hydrogen bonding.

'Non-stop fuel' – carbo-loading and endurance

Modern sports training has developed the link between correct diet and physical performance. Such interest has shown that carbohydrate-rich foods provide the most appropriate fuel for prolonged heavy exercise. Studies using samples from the muscle of athletes have shown a clear link between fatigue and reduced levels of the carbohydrate glycogen (glycogen is the main short-term energy store in the muscles, see page 48).

If an athlete in training eats a high-carbohydrate diet after exercising to exhaustion then their muscle glycogen levels recover to higher values than those existing before the exercise. This 'carbo-loading' increases by up to 50% the length of time that an athlete can exercise (*figure 4.1*). Drinking a well-formulated sports drink, containing 5–8% carbohydrate, also aids performance during sport (*figure 4.2* overleaf).

Such sports performance studies emphasise the role of carbohydrates as energy sources.

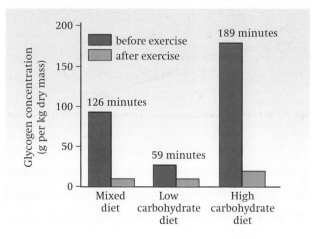

● **Figure 4.1** The results of carbo-loading. The graph shows the concentration of glycogen in muscle before and immediately after strenuous exercise for athletes following three different diets. The time recorded on the graph is the time taken to reach exhaustion. A high carbohydrate diet leads to higher glycogen levels both before and after exercise and enables athletes to exercise for longer.

● **Figure 4.2** Taking a sports drink during an endurance sport aids performance.

In this chapter we will consider the dual roles of carbohydrates – as a source of energy and as a component of physical structures in organisms.

Carbohydrates are classified according to their structure:

■ monosaccharides – simple sugars with the general formula $(CH_2O)_n$;

■ disaccharides – dimers of monosaccharides;

■ polysaccharides – polymers of monosaccharides or disaccharides.

These three types are mentioned briefly here and then discussed in more detail later in this chapter.

Monosaccharides are simple sugar molecules that provide instant-access energy to plants and animals, and act as structural units of polysaccharides. Most monosaccharides can exist as both open-chain and cyclic structures. It is the open-chain structures that will usually be given in structural formulae which follow. The formation of the cyclic structures from the open-chain structures is discussed on page 44.

■ Glucose ($C_6H_{12}O_6$) is the most important monosaccharide found in nature. As the product of photosynthesis, glucose has played a pivotal role in the development of life on Earth (*figure 4.3*). The nature of its reactivity means that the energy from the Sun trapped by photosynthesis can be easily released by the metabolic processes of respiration. Because glucose can be polymerised, its energy can be stored for later use. The human brain requires the energy from two teaspoonfuls of glucose per hour. In the diet, glucose can come from the monosaccharide itself, from some disaccharides or from starch-based foodstuffs (starch is a polysaccharide).

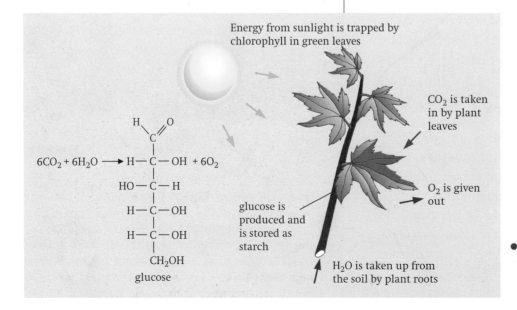

Energy from sunlight is trapped by chlorophyll in green leaves

$6CO_2 + 6H_2O \longrightarrow$ glucose $+ 6O_2$

glucose

CO_2 is taken in by plant leaves

O_2 is given out

glucose is produced and is stored as starch

H_2O is taken up from the soil by plant roots

● **Figure 4.3** A summary of photosynthesis, showing the importance of glucose.

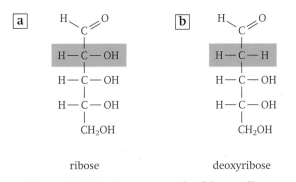

● **Figure 4.4** Some monosaccharides: **a** ribose, **b** deoxyribose. These are important components of RNA and DNA respectively.

■ Ribose and deoxyribose are found in the structure of nucleotides such as ATP (adenosine triphosphate, which is involved in energy metabolism) and also in the polymer backbone of RNA and DNA (*figure 4.4*, overleaf and chapter 6, pages 69 and 70).

■ Fructose, an isomer of glucose that contains a ketone group, is found in green plants, fruits and honey (*figure 4.5a*).

■ Mannose and galactose are two other isomers of glucose (*figures 4.5b* and *4.5c*).

Disaccharides are dimers of monosaccharides that function both as transport molecules for monosaccharides in organisms and as the structural units for some polysaccharides.

■ Lactose, formed from the reaction of the monosaccharides glucose and galactose, only occurs in the milk of mammals.

■ Maltose, which is formed from two molecules of glucose, is produced by the breakdown of starch by the enzyme amylase. Maltose also occurs in high concentration in germinating seeds.

■ Sucrose, cellobiose and trehalose are three other important disaccharides.

The structures and the nature of the bonding in these disaccharides are discussed on page 46.

Polysaccharides are condensation polymers of monosaccharides or disaccharides. They are used for energy storage and as structural components of cells. The three main polysaccharides are starch, cellulose and glycogen. All are polymers of glucose but they differ in the way that the glucose monomers are linked together (see pages 47–9).

■ Starch is an important component of our food and forms the major source of energy in the diet (*figure 4.6*). It is found naturally in vegetables and cereals, for instance.

■ Cellulose, the main structural component of plant cell walls, accounts for more than half of the carbon content of the biosphere and so is the most abundant organic compound on Earth.

■ Glycogen is an energy storage molecule in animals, where it occurs in liver cells and skeletal muscle tissue. The balance between stored glycogen and free glucose in the blood is controlled by the two hormones insulin and glucagon. Insulin promotes the conversion of glucose to glycogen, while glucagon promotes the conversion of glycogen to glucose. The illness diabetes results from a reduction in this hormonal control due to problems with the production of insulin.

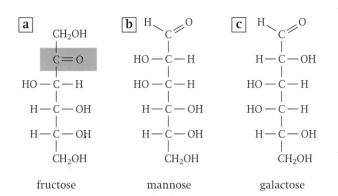

● **Figure 4.5** Some isomers of glucose: **a** fructose, **b** mannose, **c** galactose. Note the ketone group in fructose.

● **Figure 4.6** Foods containing the polysaccharide starch are very important in our diets.

Value of n	Example	Formula	Type of sugar
3	glyceraldehyde (2,3-dihydroxypropanal)	$C_3H_6O_3$	triose
4	erythrose	$C_4H_8O_4$	tetrose
5	ribose	$C_5H_{10}O_5$	pentose
6	glucose	$C_6H_{12}O_6$	hexose

● **Table 4.1** The classification of simple sugars according to chain length.

Monosaccharides

General classification of monosaccharides

Monosaccharides are aldehydes or ketones that also have two or more −OH groups (hydroxyl groups) in their structure. The general formula of these simple sugars is $(CH_2O)_n$. The value of n ranges from 3 to 9; monosaccharides can be categorised by the value of n (table 4.1).

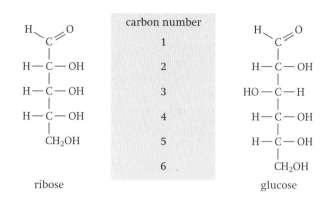

● **Figure 4.7** Open-chain structures of ribose and glucose. These structures are drawn using a set method called the Fischer projection, which enables stereoisomers to be compared easily (see *box 4A*).

Ribose is a pentose (n = 5) and glucose is a hexose (n = 6). Their open-chain structures are shown in *figure 4.7*. *Box 4A* explains how the open-chain structures of sugars, for example those drawn in *figure 4.7*, represent the real three-dimensional structures of the molecules.

SAQ 4.1

a Draw the open-chain structures of the following simple sugars:
   (i) ribose, (ii) fructose and (iii) glucose.
b State which of these monosaccharide are aldehydes and which are ketones.
c State which of these monosaccharides are pentoses and which are hexoses.

Box 4A Fischer projections

Representing in two dimensions the three-dimensional structures of open-chain monosaccharides and their various isomers requires a systematic approach. The system suggested by Emil Fischer in the 1890s is still the agreed method of drawing these structures. In a Fischer projection, a tetrahedral carbon atom is represented by two crossed lines. By convention, the horizontal lines represent bonds coming out of the page. The vertical lines represent bonds going into the page. Using molecular models is the easiest way to understand how the two-dimensional Fischer projection represents a three-dimensional structure. In fact, Emil Fischer initially developed his projection using molecular models made of toothpicks and bread rolls!

Glyceraldehyde, the simplest monosaccharide (see *table 4.1* and *box 4c*) illustrates how the system works:

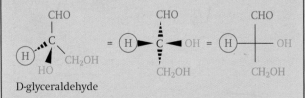

D-glyceraldehyde

In larger structures, such as ribose or glucose (see *figure 4.7*), the tetrahedral centres are simply stacked on top of each other, with the aldehyde group at the top.

SAQ 4.2

Which of the following is or are **a** a ketone, **b** an aldehyde, **c** a triose, **d** a pentose, **e** a hexose.

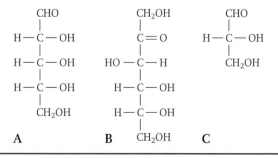

Box 4B More about monosaccharides

All the monosaccharides shown in *table 4.1*, including ribose and glucose, are aldehydes – the carbonyl group is at the end of the carbon chain. These sugars can therefore also be categorised as aldoses.

Alternatively, if the monosaccharide is a ketone, with the second carbon atom of the carbon chain being the carbonyl carbon, then the sugar is a ketose. The most significant ketose is fructose, a structural isomer of glucose (see *figure 4.5a*).

The two classifications, chain length (*n*) and type of carbonyl group, can be combined:
- ribose is an aldopentose;
- glucose is an aldohexose;
- fructose is a ketohexose.

Box 4C Stereoisomerism in simple sugars

The stereoisomerism of monosaccharides is complex. Optical isomerism and chiral centres are discussed in *Chemistry 2*, chapter 6, and in chapter 2 of this book.

Glucose has many chiral centres (marked * in *figure 4.8*). The complexity involved in describing structures with many chiral centres has led to the definition of a standard reference molecule. The reference molecule used is the simplest monosaccharide that shows optical isomerism, which is glyceraldehyde.

Glyceraldehyde has just one chiral centre, which means that it exists as two optical isomers (*figure 4.9a*). When the structure of glyceraldehyde is drawn as a Fischer projection (see *box 4A*) the isomer with the –OH group on the right of the chiral centre is the D-form and the isomer with the –OH group on the left is the L-form. This system defines two 'families' of monosaccharides. The D-sugars have the same structure as D-glyceraldehyde at the chiral carbon closest to the terminal CH_2OH of the molecule. L sugars are similarly related to L-glyceraldehyde. The structures of D- and L-glucose illustrate this system (*figure 4.9b*). In nature, D-sugars are much more abundant than L-sugars.

Monosaccharides with more than 3 carbon atoms (*n* is greater than 3) have other chiral centres. This further increases the number of stereoisomers possible for a given formula. For example, D-mannose and D-galactose are stereoisomers of D-glucose (see *figures 4.5b* and *4.5c*).

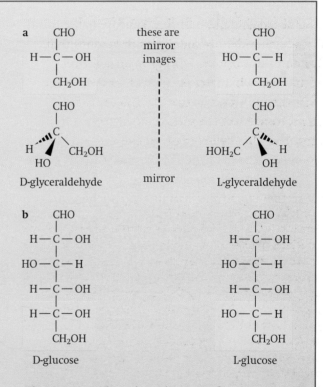

a these are mirror images

D-glyceraldehyde   mirror   L-glyceraldehyde

b

D-glucose   L-glucose

● **Figure 4.9 a** The mirror images of glyceraldehyde. **b** Two isomers of glucose, showing how the structure of glucose at carbon-5 is related to the structure of glyceraldehyde.

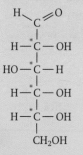

● **Figure 4.8** The open-chain structure of glucose, with * showing the four chiral centres.

Open-chain and ring structures

A hydroxyl group (–OH) can react with the carbonyl group (>C=O) of an aldehyde or a ketone by nucleophilic attack. In solution, this reaction occurs internally within a monosaccharide molecule due to the shape and flexibility of the open-chain structure. For example, in glucose a lone pair of electrons on the C-5 hydroxyl group can attack the C-1 aldehyde group (*figure 4.10*). This nucleophilic addition reaction results in the formation of a cyclic structure consisting of five carbon atoms and an oxygen atom. The six-membered ring formed from glucose is referred to as a pyranose ring. Nucleophilic addition is discussed in *Chemistry 2*, chapter 3.

The pyranose structure of glucose has a chiral centre at carbon-1. The possibility of two different orientations of the –OH group on carbon-1 produces two different isomers, known as the α form and the β form:

■ in the α-form the –OH group attached to carbon-1 is below the ring and so is on the opposite side of the ring to the –CH₂OH group on carbon-5 (*figure 4.11a*);

■ in the β-form the –OH group attached to carbon-1 is above the ring and so is on the same side of the ring as the –CH₂OH group on carbon-5 (*figure 4.11b*).

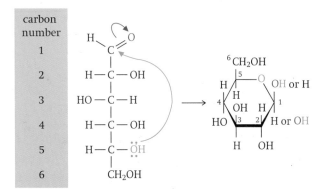

● **Figure 4.10** The formation of the pyranose ring structure of glucose.

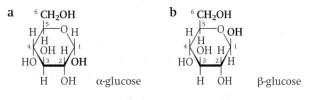

● **Figure 4.11** The α- and β-forms of glucose.

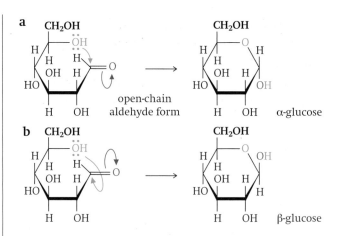

● **Figure 4.12** **a** The α-form of glucose is formed when the C-5 hydroxyl group attacks from above. **b** The β-form of glucose is formed when the C-5 hydroxyl group attacks from below.

The α-form of glucose is formed by the C-5 hydroxyl group attacking the C-1 aldehyde group from above (*figure 4.12a*). The β-form of glucose is formed when the attack is from below (*figure 4.12b*).

Crystalline D-glucose consists only of the α-form (see *box 4C* for an explanation of D and L). However, when dissolved in water, it is converted into an equilibrium mixture of 36% α-D-glucose and 64% β-D-glucose. A very small, but significant, amount of the open-chain structure is also present (*figure 4.13*). The –OH group attached to carbon-1 is particularly reactive – it is the group involved in forming bonds to other glucose molecules during the condensation reactions that produce disaccharides and polysaccharides (see below).

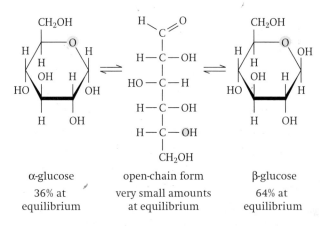

α-glucose
36% at equilibrium

open-chain form
very small amounts at equilibrium

β-glucose
64% at equilibrium

● **Figure 4.13** α-glucose, β-glucose and the open-chain structure exist in equilibrium in aqueous solution.

SAQ 4.3

Glucose is an example of an 'aldohexose' sugar which dissolves in water. In aqueous solution, glucose exists in three different structures which are in equilibrium with each other. The three structures are shown below.

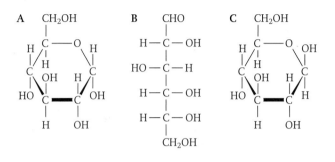

a What chemical term is used to describe the different forms shown above?
b Explain why glucose is very soluble in water.
c Which of the two cyclic forms of glucose can be described as α-glucose? Give a reason for your answer.

Disaccharides

Disaccharides are dimers in which two monosaccharide molecules are linked by a condensation reaction (*figure 4.14*). The link between the monosaccharide molecules is called a **glycosidic link**. A glycosidic link is formed by a condensation reaction between two sugar molecules. Two –OH groups react, with the elimination of a water molecule, to produce an 'oxygen bridge' between the two sugar molecules. Condensation reactions are discussed in *Chemistry 2*, chapter 3.

Two important disaccharides, maltose and cellobiose, are both dimers of glucose. The differences between them arise from how the two glucose molecules are linked.

■ In maltose, a glycosidic link is formed between carbon-1 on the first glucose molecule and carbon-4 on the second (*figure 4.15a*). The first glucose molecule (drawn on the left) is in the α-form and so the bond is an α-glycosidic link: the link in maltose is written as 1α-4. Maltose is an α-glycoside since the left-hand glucose ring is locked in the α configuration. Because carbon-1 on the right-hand ring is still free, further glucose molecules can be added and the

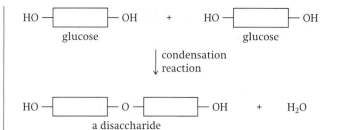

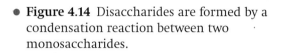

● **Figure 4.14** Disaccharides are formed by a condensation reaction between two monosaccharides.

chain can be extended to form the polysaccharide starch (see page 47).
■ Cellobiose, like maltose, is also built from two glucose molecules. However, in this case, the left-hand glucose molecule is in the β-form. A 1β-4 glycosidic link is formed between the two glucose units (*figure 4.15b*). Cellobiose is a β-glycoside since the left-hand ring is fixed in the β-form. Again, further glucose molecules can be added, to form cellulose (see page 48).
Three other disaccharides, lactose, sucrose and trehalose, are discussed in *box 4D* on page 46.

SAQ 4.4

Cellobiose and maltose are both disaccharides formed from glucose only. The structures of these two molecules are shown below.

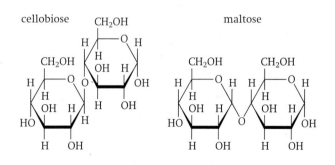

a Using these two structures, deduce two possible ring structures for the glucose molecule.
b Both cellobiose and maltose can be hydrolysed by dilute hydrochloric acid to yield glucose. However, only maltose is hydrolysed by the enzyme maltase. Explain these observations, including in your answer a balanced equation for the hydrolysis of maltose.

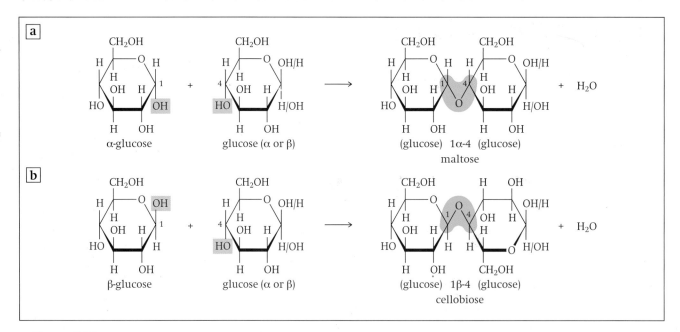

● **Figure 4.15**
a The formation of maltose, with a 1α-4 glycosidic link.
b The formation of cellobiose, with a 1β-4 glycosidic link. Note that the right-hand glucose ring in cellobiose is inverted relative to the first ring.

Box 4D More about disaccharides

Lactose, sucrose and trehalose are other important disaccharides, which are used to transport energy.

■ Carbohydrates are transferred from a mother to her infant as the disaccharide lactose in milk. Lactose is formed from galactose and glucose, joined by a 1β-4 link (*figure 4.16a*).

■ Plants usually transport sugars between tissues as concentrated solutions of sucrose. Sucrose is formed from glucose and fructose, joined by a 1α-2 link (*figure 4.16b*). When extracted and refined from sugar cane and sugar beet, sucrose is sold as table sugar.

■ Trehalose is important for the transport of sugars in insects and certain fungi. Trehalose is formed from two glucose molecules, joined by a 1α-1 link (*figure 4.16c*).

However, higher animals invariably use the monosaccharide glucose to transport energy in the bloodstream.

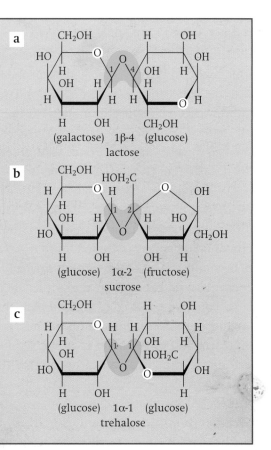

● **Figure 4.16** The structures of
a lactose,
b sucrose and
c trehalose.

The structure of polysaccharides

The differences in the structure and function of the three important polysaccharides starch, cellulose and glycogen depend largely on two features:

- the type of glycosidic link between the monomer units;
- the isomer of glucose involved in their construction.

Starch and cellulose are found in plant cells while glycogen is found in animal cells.

Polysaccharides are a further example, together with proteins and nucleic acids, of biologically important condensation polymers. You will remember that condensation polymers are built from monomers that each contain two functional groups capable of reacting to produce water (chapter 2). Each time a bond is formed between monomers, a water molecule is eliminated. In forming a polysaccharide chain, it is the −OH groups of the glucose molecules which react, and glycosidic links are formed between the monomers. Condensation polymerisation is discussed in *Chemistry 2*, chapter 7.

Starch: amylose and amylopectin

Starch exists in two forms – amylose and amylopectin. Amylose is an unbranched molecule while amylopectin is branched.

Amylose typically consists of unbranched chains of around 300 glucose units, joined by 1α-4 links (*figure 4.17*). The orientation of the rings around the 1α-4 links produces a helical molecule with six glucose units per turn (*figure 4.18*). This structure is stabilised by intramolecular hydrogen bonding involving the hydroxyl groups on

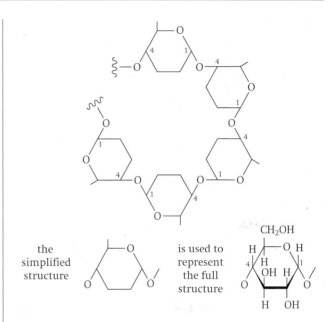

● **Figure 4.18** Amylose forms a helix due to the orientation of the 1α-4 glycosidic links. Note the simplified outline structure used for the glucose units. Hydrogen bonding helps to stabilise the helical structure.

carbon-2 and carbon-3 in each ring and the O atoms of the link and ring respectively.

Amylopectin is a branched chain polymer. The unbranched sections have the same structure as amylose, but there are numerous branches arising from 1α-6 links (*figure 4.19*). The branch points occur every 24 to 30 glucose residues along the chain. The polymer molecules are very large, involving up to a million glucose units. This makes amylopectin molecules among the largest in nature.

Starch is the storage polymer of glucose in plants. It is used as a carbohydrate store in roots, tubers, seeds and fruits. Plant cells store starch in the form of insoluble starch grains (*figure 4.20*), which contain variable amounts of the two polysaccharides, amylose (25–30%) and amylopectin (70–75%).

Starch is an important component of our food and forms the major source of energy in most diets. It is found naturally in fruit, vegetables and cereals, often in large amounts. Take a look at the contents of a range of foods from

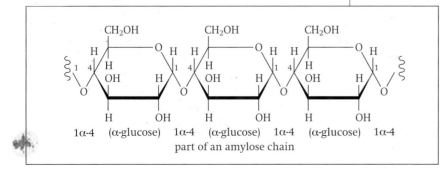

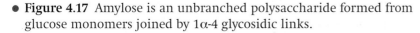

● **Figure 4.17** Amylose is an unbranched polysaccharide formed from glucose monomers joined by 1α-4 glycosidic links.

● **Figure 4.19**
Amylopectin is a branched polysaccharide. The main chain is joined by 1α-4 glycosidic links (as in amylose) and branches are linked to the main chain by 1α-6 glycosidic links. In reality a 1α-6 link is a similar length to a 1α-4 link.

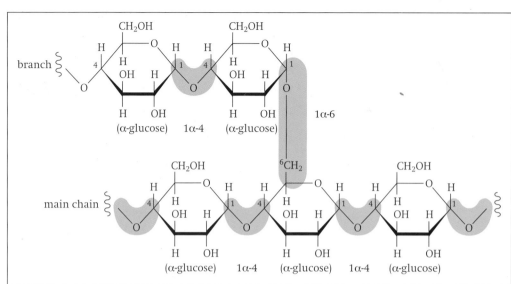

the supermarket and you will see just how important starch is (see *figure 4.6*).

The structures of amylose and amylopectin are well suited to their storage function because:

■ they are compact and do not take up much space;

■ they are insoluble and so cannot move out of the cells in which they are stored;

■ they enable a very large number of glucose units to be stored within cells without generating a high osmotic pressure (osmotic pressure is a property dependent on the number of solute particles present in a solution – if a large number of glucose monomers were present inside the cell, the net flow of water molecules into the cell would burst it);

● **Figure 4.20** A photomicrograph of starch grains from a potato, × 800.

■ they do not become involved in the immediate metabolic processes of the cells;

■ they are easily hydrolysed by enzymes to soluble sugars when required (see page 50).

Starch is an important part of the diet of livestock, both in the grass they eat and in their food supplements. It is also important for a healthy diet in humans because it is digested slowly and releases glucose progressively.

Worldwide, about 30 million tonnes of starch are obtained from plants each year. Perhaps surprisingly, most of this starch is used for industrial purposes! These uses include making glues, wallpaper paste, paper and card coatings, carbon paper, corrugated board, textiles, paints, packaging and insulating materials, biodegradable plastics and rubber. Various different forms of starch are used to make high-value products such as cosmetics and medicines, and even a form of concrete.

Cellulose – the structural carbohydrate of plant cell walls

Plant cells have a rigid cell wall that supports and protects the cell. Cellulose fibres are the major structural component of the material that forms the cell wall.

Cellulose is an unbranched polymer of up to 15 000 β-glucose monomers linked by 1β-4 glycosidic bonds (*figure 4.21*). Due to the orientation of the glucose units the molecules do not coil into a helical shape, but form a linear molecule. Parallel neighbouring chains are able to interact with each other by cross-linked hydrogen bonds. Up to 60 or 70 individual chains can be held together to form a column known as a microfibril (*figure 4.22*). Bundles consisting of many microfibrils are assembled together to form the cellulose fibres which give tensile strength to the cell wall.

Glycogen – 'animal starch'

Glycogen is an energy storage molecule in animals, where it occurs in liver cells and muscle tissue (*figure 4.23*). The structure of glycogen is very similar to amylopectin (see *figure 4.19*), but glycogen is more extensively branched. The unbranched sections are formed from glucose molecules linked by 1α-4 glycosidic bonds. At the branch points, 1α-6 glycosidic bonds are found. In

glycogen the branching points occur every 8 to 12 residues and the branches are shorter. Glycogen forms a very compact structure.

Polysaccharides – storage and structural carbohydrates

The structures of the three main polysaccharides, cellulose, starch and glycogen, have been discussed above. For all three, their structure is closely related to their function. *Table 4.2* summarises the features of the three main polysaccharides.

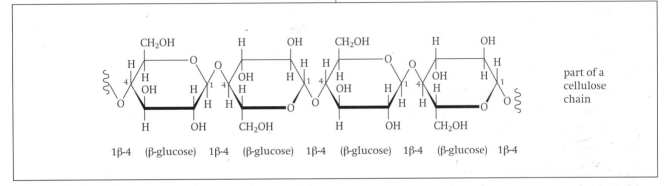

part of a cellulose chain

1β-4 (β-glucose) 1β-4 (β-glucose) 1β-4 (β-glucose) 1β-4 (β-glucose) 1β-4

- **Figure 4.21** Cellulose is an unbranched polysaccharide formed from β-glucose monomers joined by 1β-4 glycosidic links. The inversion of one sugar unit in relation to the next results in a linear molecule.

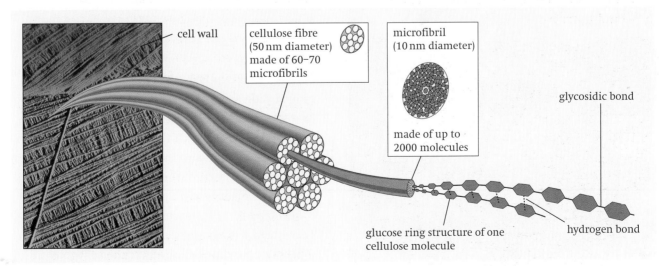

cell wall

cellulose fibre (50 nm diameter) made of 60–70 microfibrils

microfibril (10 nm diameter)

made of up to 2000 molecules

glycosidic bond

glucose ring structure of one cellulose molecule

hydrogen bond

- **Figure 4.22** Cellulose chains can be held together by hydrogen bonds to form bundles. 60–70 of these bundles can pack together to produce a cellulose microfibril and thence a fibre for use in structures such as plant cell walls.

Polysaccharide		Monomer	Type of glycosidic link	Shape of macromolecule	Function
starch	amylose	α-glucose	1α-4	unbranched chains wound into a helix	carbohydrate storage in plants
	amylopectin	α-glucose	1α-4 and also 1α-6 at branches	tightly packed branched chains	carbohydrate storage in plants
glycogen		α-glucose	1α-4 and also 1α-6 at branches	very branched, compact molecules	carbohydrate storage in animals
cellulose		β-glucose	1β-4	linear	structural in plant cell walls

● **Table 4.2** A summary of the features of the major polysaccharides.

Hydrolysis of sugars

Hydrolysis is the reverse of the condensation reaction that forms disaccharides and polysaccharides. Covalent bonds are broken during hydrolysis, with water (as H and OH) being added to the fragments.

$$\text{monosaccharides} \underset{\text{hydrolysis}}{\overset{\substack{\text{condensation}\\ \text{polymerisation}}}{\rightleftharpoons}} \substack{\text{disaccharides or}\\ \text{polysaccharides}} + \text{water}$$

Acid hydrolysis

Hydrolysis of disaccharides or polysaccharides can be brought about by warming (70 °C) with dilute hydrochloric acid (1 mol dm^{-3}). Acid hydrolysis of

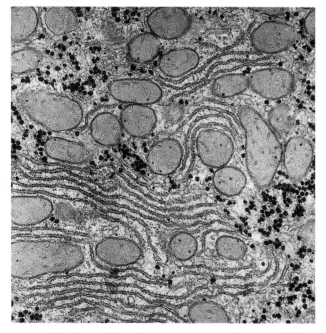

● **Figure 4.23** An electronmicrograph of glycogen granules (black dots) in liver cells. Glycogen is also stored in skeletal muscle.

polysaccharides can be used in analysing the structure of complex carbohydrates. The hydrolysis is usually followed up by chemical testing and then paper chromatography is used to find the nature of the monomers present in the structure. (Paper chromatography of the products of protein hydrolysis is discussed in chapter 2, *box 2B*, page 20)

Acid hydrolysis of starch can also be used as a source of glucose in the food industry. An example of this is the production of sweetening syrup. Glucose itself is not as sweet as fructose and so the glucose produced by acid hydrolysis is converted to fructose using immobilised glucose isomerase (see chapter 3, page 34).

Enzyme hydrolysis of carbohydrates

Biological systems require the hydrolysis of specific glycosidic bonds. Plants and animals have enzyme systems for the controlled hydrolysis of stored starch or glycogen, respectively, while starch taken in by animals as food can also be hydrolysed.

In humans, the digestion of starch begins in the mouth. Saliva contains an α-amylase, an enzyme that specifically hydrolyses 1α-4 glycosidic bonds. Digestion of starch with this enzyme produces a mixture of glucose and maltose. This enzyme cannot break bonds in the region of the branching points in amylopectin. A pancreatic α-amylase continues to digest starch in the small intestine. This enzyme is again specific for 1α-4 links.

Human amylases cannot hydrolyse β-glycosidic links. Because of this, we cannot digest cellulose. Any cellulose in our diet acts as dietary fibre. This has the beneficial effect of providing bulk to our food and helping its passage through the digestive system.

Despite the abundance of cellulose in nature, cellulase enzymes are rare and most animals cannot utilise cellulose as food. However, some bacteria and fungi are able to synthesise such an enzyme. Animals such as cows and sheep have bacteria in their stomachs that produce a cellulase to break down cellulose. These mammals can use grass and hay as food; they then absorb the monosaccharides and disaccharides released by the bacteria (*figure 4.24*).

Carbohydrate solubility

All the different carbohydrates contain a significant number of –OH groups. For the monosaccharides and disaccharides, the –OH groups are an important factor in their solubility since they form hydrogen bonds with water molecules (*figure 4.25*). This solubility enables small sugar molecules to be transported and metabolised readily.

In contrast with monosaccharides and disaccharides, an essential part of the function of polysaccharides is that they are not readily soluble in water.

- In cellulose, the linear molecules interact strongly with one another, forming fibrous structures that are insoluble in water. Although there are many –OH groups, they tend to be on

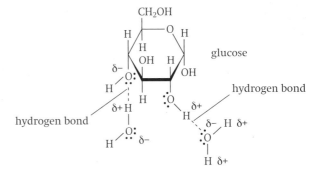

- **Figure 4.25** Glucose is soluble in water due to the formation of hydrogen bonds.

the inside of the fibres and are involved in internal hydrogen bonding between the chains. As a result, the interactions of the polymeric chains with water are restricted.

- Neither amylose nor amylopectin are truly soluble in water. The –OH groups in the unbranched, coiled chains of amylose are more accessible to water than those of the more compact, branched amylopectin chains. Thus there is more scope for hydrogen bonding with water in the case of amylose. As a result, amylose is the more soluble polymer of the two.
- Glycogen is even more branched than amylopectin and is likewise only sparingly soluble.

Cooking a rice or pasta dish illustrates the effect of water on carbohydrate polymers (*figure 4.26*). As the pasta or rice is heated in water, it swells as the polymer chains become hydrated. However, although swollen, the polymer chains do not dissolve away.

- **Figure 4.24** Cows can use cellulose as food. This is because cows have bacteria in their stomachs that break down cellulose to glucose – this is what happens when cows chew the cud.

- **Figure 4.26** Equal amounts of rice shown before and after cooking. The increase in volume shows how much water is absorbed by carbohydrate polymers during the cooking process.

SAQ 4.5

The diagram below shows a part of the structure of a carbohydrate storage polymer which can be broken down by enzyme action.

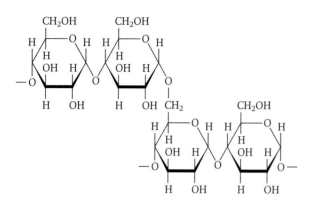

a What types of glycosidic linkage are present in this structure?

b Name this type of breakdown reaction.

c Draw the structure of the monomer unit produced.

d Suggest which carbohydrate polymer this drawing represents.

e Suggest why the polysaccharide functions as an energy store but the monomer does not.

SAQ 4.6

Describe the difference in structure between starch and cellulose. How does this difference affect human nutrition?

SUMMARY

- The simplest carbohydrates are monosaccharides. The general formula of these simple sugars is $(CH_2O)_n$. Such molecules are aldehydes or ketones that also contain two or more hydroxyl (−OH) groups.

- Simple sugars contain chiral carbon atoms.

- Simple sugars, such as glucose, can exist in open-chain and cyclic structures. In aqueous solution most glucose exists in the cyclic structure. There are two cyclic isomers of glucose, α-glucose and β-glucose. These differ in the orientation of the −OH group attached to carbon-1 in the ring structure.

- Simple sugar molecules can form dimers, known as disaccharides.

- Maltose and cellobiose are both made from two glucose molecules; however, the glucose molecules are joined differently. Maltose contains a 1α-4 glycosidic bond, whereas cellobiose contains a 1β-4 glycosidic bond.

- Polysaccharides are condensation polymers that have storage and structural functions in organisms.

- Amylose is an unbranched polymer of glucose molecules linked by 1α-4 glycosidic bonds.

- Amylopectin is a branched polymer. The unbranched parts of the molecule are similar to amylose, but there are numerous branches arising from 1α-6 glycosidic links. Amylopectin molecules are among the largest in nature but the brush-like structure is very compact.

- Starch is the storage form of glucose in plants. It contains variable amounts of the two polysaccharides, amylose and amylopectin, depending on the source of the starch. Amylose and amylopectin function to store very large numbers of glucose molecules.

- Cellulose fibres are the major structural component of plant cell walls. Cellulose is an unbranched polymer of β-glucose monomers linked by 1β-4 glycosidic bonds.

- Cellulose is linear because of the orientation of the glucose units. The rod-like molecules are held together by hydrogen bonds and assemble into cellulose fibres. These give tensile strength to the plant cell wall.

- Glycogen is the energy storage molecule in animals and has a very similar structure to amylopectin but more branches occur.

- Polysaccharides are easily hydrolysed to simple sugars.

- The hydrolysis of polysaccharides can be achieved by warming with dilute hydrochloric acid.

- Polysaccharides can also be hydrolysed by enzymes, which convert polysaccharides to monosaccharides when required. Thus the energy stored in these molecules is readily accessible to the organism.

- Simple sugars such as glucose are readily soluble in water because of hydrogen bonding to water molecules through the sugar hydroxyl groups.

- The hydroxyl groups in polysaccharides are involved in hydrogen bonds between the polymer chains. Therefore, the polysaccharides are insoluble. Starch and glycogen are stored in granules within cells. Cellulose forms extracellular fibres.

Questions

1 Glucose is a simple sugar of formula $C_6H_{12}O_6$. In aqueous solution, glucose exists mostly in a cyclic form. The molecule drawn here is the α-form.

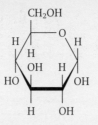

a Draw the molecule in the β-form.

b Both the α- and β- forms of glucose form condensation polymers of biological importance.

(i) Name a polysaccharide formed from glucose in the α-form and give its biological function.

(ii) Name a polysaccharide formed from β-glucose and describe its biological function.

c A human being was fed glucose in which some of the carbon atoms were the radioactive isotope ^{14}C, and some of the hydrogen atoms were tritium (^3H). The waste products from the person were analysed.

(i) Why do you think that glucose was used in which only **some** of the carbon and hydrogen atoms had been replaced with their radioactive isotopes?

(ii) Which major radioactive compounds would be produced by the person? Explain your answers.

2 The diagrams on the left represent the structure of some common carbohydrates.

a Suggest a suitable identity for each of the structures A, B, C, and D.

b Given that the chemical formula for glucose is $C_6H_{12}O_6$ write down the equation to show the production of the disaccharide maltose.

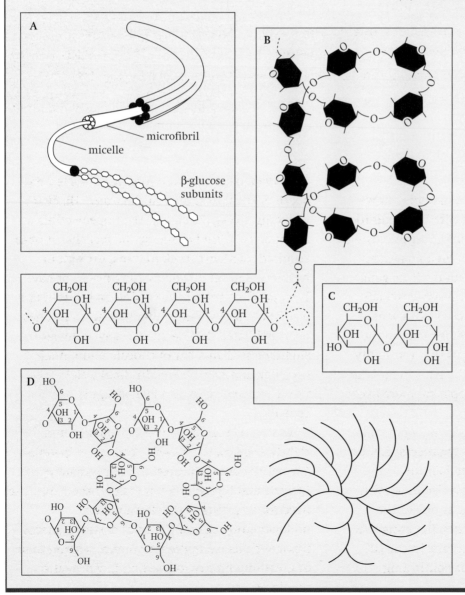

CHAPTER 5

Lipids and membranes

By the end of this chapter you should be able to:

1 describe the structure and function of triglyceryl esters (triglycerides);

2 describe the *hydrolysis* of triglycerides as a source of fatty acids, for example in soap-making;

3 explain the *solubility* of triglycerides in non-polar solvents;

4 describe the structure and function of phosphoglycerides in the formation of *bimolecular layers*;

5 explain that *lipids*, treated simply as $(CH_2)_n$, are essentially a concentrated energy store of carbon and hydrogen;

6 explain that *carbohydrates*, treated simply as $(CH_2O)_n$, are made up of partly oxidised carbon and hydrogen units, allowing more 'instant access' to energy;

7 explain why, on complete oxidation, lipids release more energy per gram than carbohydrates do.

An epidemic of obesity

Fat is an important part of the human diet, as we shall see in this chapter. Among tribal communities in Africa a normal cycle of accumulating and using body fat can be demonstrated. Immediately after harvest each year everyone in a rural village gains weight. Most adults double their reserves of body fat at this time. This fat is then used to prevent starvation when food stores diminish later in the year. This natural cycle reminds us that the ability to lay down stores of energy in the form of fat is an evolutionary advantage – fat people are more likely to survive a famine.

With supermarkets and restaurants open at all hours and much food now highly processed, most modern societies have eliminated famine. However, the penalty for this is a rise in obesity. Obesity now ranks with asthma as one of the fastest-growing medical epidemics afflicting the West. The proportion of obese adults in the UK doubled during the 1980s and is continuing to rise.

In 1995, newspapers in America reported the death of the fattest man in the world. He died weighing 465 kg (73 stone). The tragedy of his situation was emphasised by the fact that it once required a fork-lift truck to transport him to hospital. And yet, his over-eating need not have been particularly excessive. If he had started at a weight of 70 kg when he was 16 years old, it has been estimated that he merely needed to eat slightly less than a bar of chocolate too much each day in order to reach his final weight. His was an extreme case of a loss of regulatory control.

Most of us regulate our body weight more tightly. Even so, the growing number of people becoming obese indicates that our sedentary lifestyle and high-fat diet are taking their toll. The need for scientists to develop a greater understanding of how the body balances energy input with its energy requirements is going to be of great importance in averting major health problems.

Lipids

Lipids are a varied group of biochemical compounds, but they are grouped together because of their non-polar nature. Lipids are largely insoluble in water, but are soluble in non-polar solvents such as hexane. Lipid molecules are not polymers but their non-polar nature means that they tend to group together when placed in water.

Lipids play essential roles in cell structure and metabolism. Biochemically important lipids include the following: triglycerides, phosphoglycerides and steroids.

- **Triglycerides** occur in animal fats, which are solid at room temperature, and vegetable oils, which are liquid at room temperature. Triglycerides are the major storage form of the energy needed to drive reactions in plants and animals. *Figure 5.1* shows the structure of a typical triglyceride.
- **Phosphoglycerides** are important constituents of cell membranes. *Figure 5.2* shows the structure of a typical phosphoglyceride.
- **Steroids** are another series of biologically important molecules (see *box 5A*).

Triglycerides

Structure of triglycerides

Triglycerides are formed by the addition of three **fatty acid** molecules to a molecule of propane-1,2,3-triol (*figure 5.4*). Fatty acid molecules

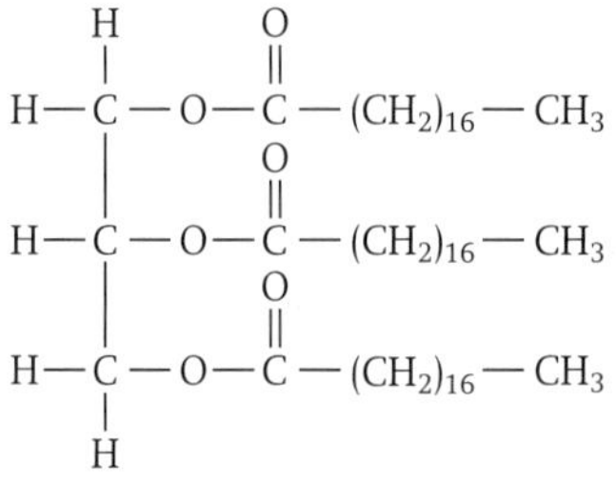

● **Figure 5.1** A representative triglyceride.

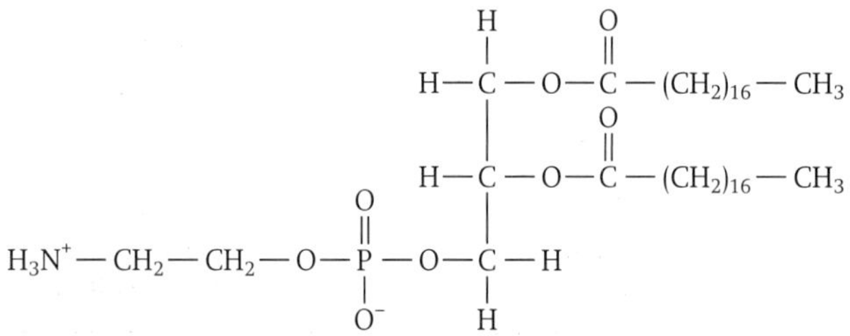

● **Figure 5.2** A representative phosphoglyceride.

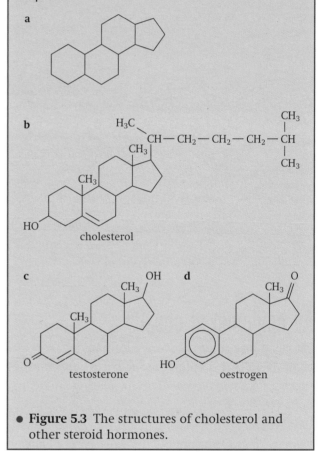

Box 5A Steroids

Steroids are based on a structure of four alicyclic hydrocarbon rings (*figure 5.3a*). They do not contain long-chain carboxylic acids. However, they are classified as lipids.

Cholesterol (*figure 5.3b*) is present in food and is also manufactured in the liver. Animals synthesise other steroids from cholesterol. These steroids include the male and female sex hormones (*figures 5.3c* and *5.3d*), certain vitamins and the bile acids that assist in the digestion of lipids.

cholesterol

testosterone   oestrogen

● **Figure 5.3** The structures of cholesterol and other steroid hormones.

consist of long, non-polar hydrocarbon chains with a carboxylic acid group (–COOH) at one end. (Carboxylic acids are discussed in *Chemistry 2*, chapter 4.) The hydrocarbon chains are

propane-1,2,3-triol

● **Figure 5.4** Structural formula and model of propane-1,2,3-triol (commonly known as glycerol).

unbranched and have an even number of carbon atoms. In higher plants and animals most of the fatty acids in triglycerides have chains of 16 or 18 carbon atoms (*figure 5.5* and *table 5.1*).

The reaction that links the fatty acids to propane-1,2,3-triol in a triglyceride is a condensation reaction known as **esterification** (*figure 5.6*). (Esterification is discussed in *Chemistry 2*, chapter 4.)

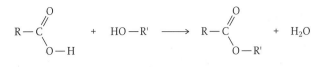

● **Figure 5.6** An esterification reaction.

Common name	Systematic name	Principal source	Melting point (°C)
palmitic acid	hexadecanoic acid	animal fats, especially cow's milk, and palm oil	63.0
stearic acid	octadecanoic acid	animal fats	69.5
oleic acid	*cis*-octadeca-9-enoic acid	olive oil	13.4
linoleic acid	*cis,cis*-octadeca-9,12-dienoic acid	sunflower oil	−5

● **Table 5.1** Examples of some fatty acids.

Simple triglycerides contain three molecules of one particular fatty acid bonded to one molecule of propane-1,2,3-triol. For example, tristearin, which is found in the fatty tissue of animals, is formed from propane-1,2,3-triol and three molecules of stearic acid (*figure 5.7*).

Most naturally occurring triglyceride molecules are mixed triglycerides; they have two or three different fatty acids attached to the propane-1,2,3-triol molecule. The fatty acid composition varies with the organism that produces them.

The major distinction in the fatty acid composition of triglycerides is between saturated and unsaturated fatty acids:

■ saturated fatty acids, such as palmitic acid and stearic acid, possess only C–C single bonds in their chains (see *figure 5.5* and *Chemistry 1*, chapter 9);

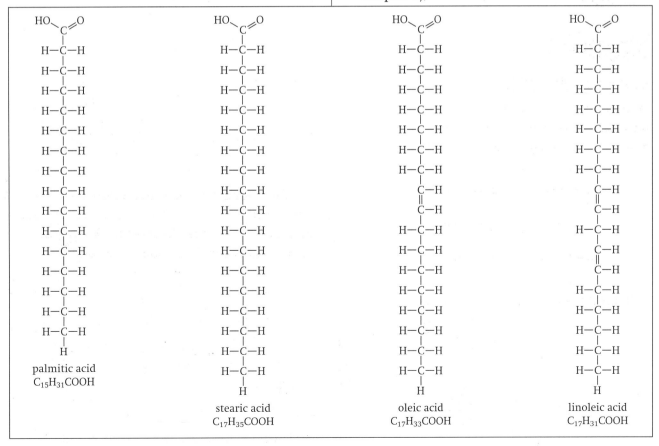

● **Figure 5.5** Structural formulae of palmitic acid, stearic acid, oleic acid and linoleic acid.

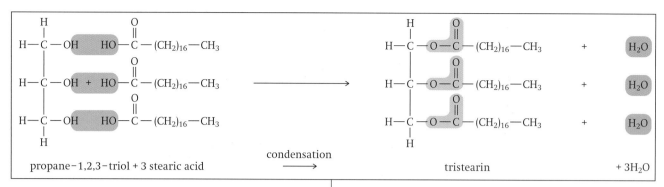

propane−1,2,3−triol + 3 stearic acid $\xrightarrow{\text{condensation}}$ tristearin + 3H₂O

- **Figure 5.7** The formation of tristearin from propane-1,2,3-triol and stearic acid.

- unsaturated fatty acids, such as oleic acid and linoleic acid, have one or more C=C double bonds per chain (see *figure 5.5* and *Chemistry 1*, chapter 10).

Unsaturated fatty acids tend to have lower melting points than saturated fatty acids (see *table 5.1*). This seems to be a significant factor in influencing the triglyceride composition produced by different organisms.

Animal fats are usually richer in saturated fatty acids than plant oils are. In warm-blooded animals, body temperature is high enough to allow most fats to be above their melting temperature. This means they can be transported around the body as liquids. These fats tend to be highly saturated, with a high content of palmitic acid and stearic acid.

Plants have no means of keeping themselves warm when faced with cold conditions. Plant oils must therefore have lower melting points and are often highly unsaturated. They contain high proportions of oleic acid and linoleic acid.

Fish oils are highly unsaturated for similar reasons. They can contain long fatty acid groups with as many as six C=C bonds.

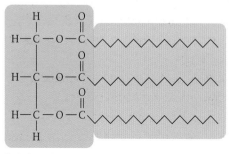

slightly polar 'head'　　non-polar 'tail'

- **Figure 5.8** Triglycerides have a slightly polar 'head' and a long non-polar 'tail'.

In summary, a triglyceride molecule consists of:
- a slightly polar region or 'head', formed from the propane-1,2,3-triol molecule and the ester groups;
- a non-polar 'tail', formed by the three long-chain fatty acids (*figure 5.8*).

Hydrolysis of triglycerides

Vegetable oils and animal fats can develop an unpleasant smell if they are kept for too long. They are said to go rancid. Fatty acids formed through the hydrolysis of triglycerides are the cause of this rancidity. This hydrolysis is speeded up by the presence of certain micro-organisms. Some of the fatty acids released are volatile, and some have distinctly unpleasant odours and flavours. An example is butanoic acid, which is formed when butter fat is hydrolysed. This type of rancidity is known as hydrolytic rancidity.

Not all examples of hydrolysis are detrimental. There is an increasing interest in using vegetable oils in a wide variety of circumstances, ranging from healthier foodstuffs to renewable fuels. Since it is the fatty acid component of triglycerides that varies from one source to another, isolating the fatty acids by hydrolysis is the first stage in the analysis of triglycerides. The fatty acids present in the different oils are separated and analysed by a variety of chromatography techniques.

The hydrolysis of triglycerides is commercially important in the manufacture of soaps. Soft, 'toilet' soaps are generally made by hydrolysing the triglyceryl esters present in a blend of animal fats and vegetable oils by heating them with a solution of sodium hydroxide. Hydrolysis yields propane-1,2,3-triol and the sodium salts of the fatty acids (*figure 5.9*). This process is known as **saponification** (which means soap-making).

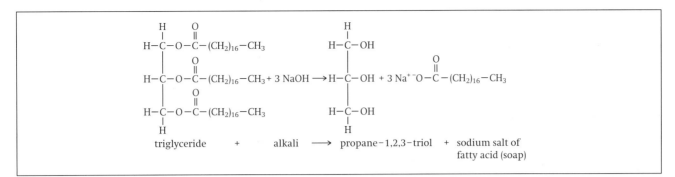

● **Figure 5.9** An equation showing the saponification of a triglyceride.

Solubility of triglycerides

The non-polar nature of the hydrocarbon chains overwhelms any polarity a triglyceride might have due to the oxygen atoms in the ester links. As a result, triglycerides do not dissolve in or mix with water as they have no capacity to interact with water molecules through hydrogen bonding.

The long hydrocarbon chains do, however, offer scope for the formation of instantaneous dipole–induced dipole interactions (van der Waals' forces) with organic solvents. The possibility of such interactions means that triglycerides are soluble in non-polar hydrocarbon solvents such as hexane. The interactions involved here are between instantaneous dipoles created by changes in the distribution of electrons within

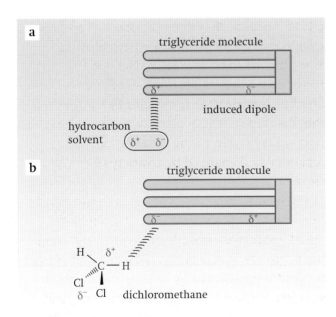

● **Figure 5.10** Triglycerides dissolve in **a** hydrocarbon and **b** polar organic solvents.

the molecules (see *figure 5.10a* and *Chemistry 1*, chapter 3).

Triglycerides are also soluble in polar organic solvents, such as halogenoalkanes, and ethers, such as dichloromethane and ethoxyethane. Here the solvent molecule possesses a permanent dipole, which induces a dipole in the triglyceride molecule (*figure 5.10b*). The resulting interaction contributes to the solubility of the triglyceride in the solvent. Halogenoalkane solvents are the type of solvent used by dry-cleaners to remove grease and stains from clothes.

SAQ 5.1

a Explain the meaning of the following terms: (i) lipid, (ii) triglyceride, (iii) unsaturated fatty acid and (iv) saturated fatty acid.

b If too much glucose is absorbed by organisms, some of the excess is converted into fatty acids. One such fatty acid is palmitic acid, which has the formula $C_{15}H_{31}COOH$.
   (i) Write down the formula of the triglyceride derived from palmitic acid and propane-1,2,3-triol.
   (ii) What name is given to the type of link that joins the fatty acid to propane-1,2,3-triol?
   (iii) Is this compound likely to be solid or liquid at room temperature?

c (i) Write a structural formula for the mixed triglyceride molecule formed from propane-1,2,3-triol, hexadecanoic acid, octadecanoic acid and octadeca-9,12-dienoic acid.
   (ii) Write the equation for the saponification of this triglyceride.

Phosphoglycerides

All cells are surrounded by a membrane which controls the exchange of chemicals, such as food and waste products, between the cell and its environment. Membranes are also present within cells, where they surround the various internal compartments. The major lipid component of these **cell membranes** is **phosphoglycerides**.

Phosphoglycerides contain a charged phosphate group and so are often referred to as polar lipids. Propane-1,2,3-triol forms the backbone of a phosphoglyceride molecule, and two long-chain fatty acids are attached to C-1 and C-2 of the propane-1,2,3-triol backbone by ester links. The third position is occupied by a substituted phosphate group, attached by an ester link (*figure 5.11*). This phosphate group is attached, also via an ester link, to the −OH group of a small polar molecule (represented by X in *figure 5.11*). X can come from a molecule such as choline, ethanolamine or serine (*figure 5.12*).

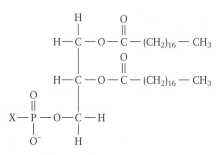

● **Figure 5.11** The generalised structure of a phosphoglyceride molecule.

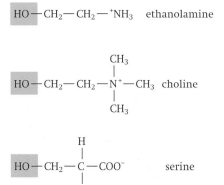

● **Figure 5.12** Some of the X groups that may form part of a phosphoglyceride molecule.

In summary, a phosphoglyceride molecule consists of:

■ a polar region or 'head', formed from the phosphate group and the attached polar molecule (X in *figure 5.11*);

■ a non-polar 'tail', formed by the two long-chain fatty acids (*figure 5.13*).

The two non-polar long-chain fatty groups of a phosphoglyceride interact together through van der Waals' forces and lie in the same direction. The polar phosphate group points in the opposite direction.

SAQ 5.2

a Name the elements present in (i) a triglyceride and (ii) a phosphoglyceride.

b Describe briefly, with the aid of diagrams, the major structural differences between triglyceride and phosphoglyceride molecules.

Lipids and cell membranes

Self-assembly – monolayers and micelles

Even though they are electrically neutral molecules, triglyceride molecules do have distinct charged regions in their structure. The long hydrocarbon chains are non-polar. The terminal, ester linkage region is slightly polar (see *figure 5.8*). The presence of oxygen atoms in the ester link means that the ester link can interact with water molecules through hydrogen bonding, but not sufficiently to cause the triglyceride molecule to dissolve. When placed on the surface of water, a

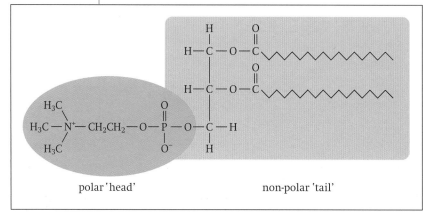

polar 'head'   non-polar 'tail'

● **Figure 5.13** Phosphoglycerides have a polar 'head' and a long non-polar 'tail'.

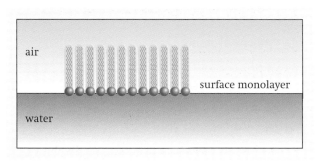

● **Figure 5.14** A triglyceride monolayer formed on water.

liquid triglyceride forms a **monolayer** in which the non-polar hydrocarbon tails extend into the air (away from the water) and the polar head is in the water (*figure 5.14*).

If enough triglyceride molecules are present, they can group together to form spherical structures known as micelles. In these structures, the polar heads of the triglyceride molecules face out into the water, and the non-polar tails group together in the centre of the sphere, away from the water (*figure 5.15*). This process is a simple example of **self-assembly**.

Bimolecular layers

Triglycerides do not form structures more complicated than the simple micelles shown in *figure 5.15*. This is because of the bulk of the three hydrocarbon chains in a triglyceride molecule. However, the structure of phosphoglycerides, with two hydrocarbon chains forming the non-polar 'tail', is more rectangular. Structures formed from phosphoglycerides can be enlarged to contain sections where the molecules are arranged in a **bimolecular layer** (*figure 5.16*).

These bimolecular layers can take different forms.

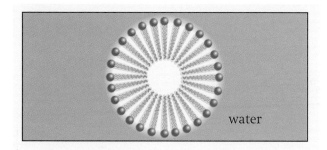

● **Figure 5.15** The structure of a micelle formed from triglycerides.

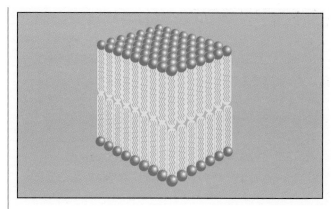

● **Figure 5.16** A bimolecular layer formed from phosphoglycerides in water.

■ The packing together of phosphoglycerides in aqueous suspension gives rise to disc-shaped micelles that are really extended bimolecular layers (*figure 5.17*).

■ If a concentrated suspension of phosphoglycerides in water is subjected to ultrasonic vibrations then structures are formed that contain water inside, bounded by only a single bimolecular layer (*figure 5.18*). This type of structure has been used as a model of cell membranes (*box 5B*).

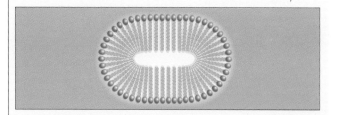

● **Figure 5.17** The structure of a disc-shaped micelle formed from phosphoglycerides in water can be considered to be an extended bimolecular layer.

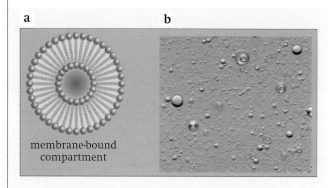

● **Figure 5.18** Phosphoglycerides can form structures that contain water within the bimolecular layer. **a** schematic, **b** electron micrograph (× 1000) showing many liposomes.

Box 5B The fluid mosaic model of cell membranes

The role of cell membranes in separating the various compartments of a cell is important, but fully evolved cell membranes also perform other major functions. These include the transport of chemicals in and out of the cell and recognition of 'signal' molecules such as hormones and neurotransmitters.

Analysis of cell membranes shows that their composition varies with cell type and location. However, an approximate ratio of 40% lipid to 60% protein is common. *Figure 5.19* shows an electronmicrograph of a cell membrane.

Our current model for the structure of membranes is the fluid mosaic model. The phosphoglyceride bimolecular layer forms the core of the structure. The phosphoglycerides are able to move from side to side, giving the cell flexibility, while cholesterol molecules are present to give the membrane greater rigidity. The phosphoglycerides also give the cells high electrical resistance and impermeability to highly polar molecules. A 'mosaic' of proteins is embedded in the bimolecular layer. Proteins can be located in one or other of the membrane surfaces, or span the whole membrane from one surface to the other (*figure 5.20*).

● **Figure 5.19** An electronmicrograph of a cell, showing the bimolecular layer that forms the cell membrane (× 130 000).

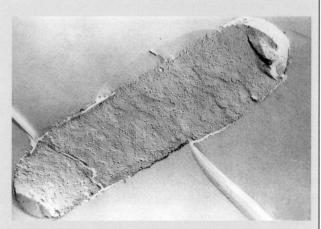

● **Figure 5.20** A freeze-etched, high magnification electronmicrograph of a cell membrane, showing the 'mosaic' of proteins in the bimolecular layer (× 25 000).

Factor	Glycogen	Triglycerides (fats)
efficiency	efficient, relatively short-term, concentrated energy store	highly efficient, long-term, concentrated energy store
storage	compact, insoluble polymer molecules, stored in granules	triglyceride molecules are completely insoluble, aggregate together in droplets
need for hydrolysis	glycogen chains readily hydrolysed to glucose prior to oxidation	triglycerides readily hydrolysed to free, long-chain acids prior to oxidation
energy per mole	glucose molecules from glycogen are already partially oxidised, containing oxygen atoms – they can be regarded as having the formula $(CHOH)_n$ – so: ■ provide more instant access to energy than fats ■ produce less energy per mole than fats	long-chain acid molecules represent carbon and hydrogen in a highly reduced form – they can be regarded as having the formula $(CH_2)_n$ – so: ■ produce more energy per mole than glucose ■ also release more water when metabolised (known as metabolic water, this is important in dry climates).
need for oxygen	glucose molecules are already partially oxidised, so can be metabolised under anaerobic conditions to produce some energy	triglycerides cannot be metabolised under anaerobic conditions – energy cannot be released in the absence of oxygen

● **Table 5.2** Comparison of glycogen and triglycerides as energy stores.

Lipids and energy

A person's supply of glycogen (chapter 4) acts as a relatively short-term energy store; it can provide energy for less than 24 hours. Triglycerides are the longer-term energy store in the human body. The fat content of an average person in the West (21% for men, 26% for women) enables them to survive starvation for 2 to 3 months. *Table 5.2* summarises the main features of glycogen and fats as energy stores. *Table 5.3* in *box 5C* shows that triglycerides can store slightly more than twice as much energy as the same dry mass of glycogen.

In animals, triglycerides are synthesised and stored in specialised fat cells (*figure 5.21*). These cells can be almost entirely filled with fat globules, unlike other cell types that contain only a few droplets of fat. Triglycerides, being weakly polar molecules, are stored in anhydrous form. In con-

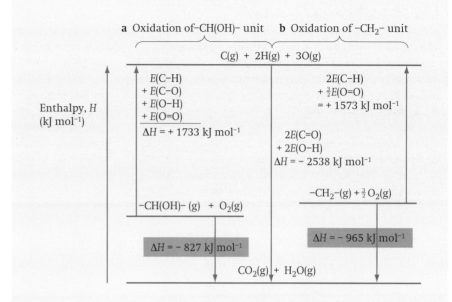

● **Figure 5.22** Energy level diagrams, showing that –CH(OH)– (i.e. carbohydrates, **a**) releases less energy than –CH$_2$– (i.e. fatty acids, **b**) when oxidised to CO_2 and H_2O.

trast, glycogen binds about twice its weight of water. Because of this, under the conditions found in the body, fats provide about six times the metabolic energy of an equal weight of hydrated glycogen.

Triglycerides store energy in a highly efficient form. However, unlike glycogen, they cannot produce energy when muscles are starved of oxygen (anaerobic conditions), for example during extreme exercise such as sprinting. This means that both glycogen and triglycerides are required for humans to function properly.

Fats are a highly efficient form in which to store energy because they can be regarded essentially as long hydrocarbon chains made up of –CH$_2$– units. Carbohydrates, in contrast, contain a much higher proportion of oxygen. They can be regarded as molecules made up of –CH(OH)– units. Carbohydrates are already partly oxidised and therefore give less energy when converted to carbon dioxide (CO_2) and water (H_2O).

This difference can be illustrated by comparing the energy diagrams for the oxidation of the two basic units (*figure 5.22*). Using bond enthalpies it is possible to estimate the difference between the energy given out in the two cases. Do note that this is only an illustration as the values we are considering are for changes in the gaseous phase.

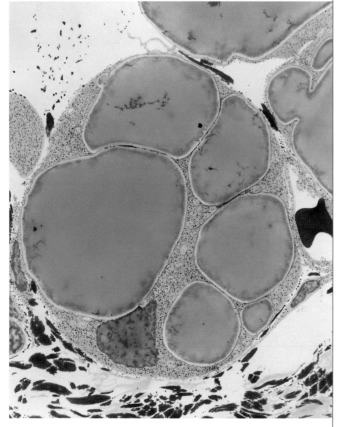

● **Figure 5.21** Fat cells filled with fat globules.

Box 5C Triglycerides and diet

Each year the Earth's human population uses 80 million tonnes of fats and oils. This vast consumption of natural resources provides raw materials for the manufacture of both non-edible products (soaps, detergents and cosmetics) and edible products. Edible products high in fat include:

- cooking fat;
- frying oils;
- margarine and similar spreads;
- dairy products (butter, cheese, cream);
- salad oils and mayonnaise;
- snack foods (for example ice cream, chocolates and nuts).

Table 5.3 shows the energy content of the three major food constituents: fat, carbohydrate and protein.

A high consumption of saturated fats has been linked to high blood concentrations of cholesterol and to an increased risk of coronary heart disease. However, it would appear that products based on olive oil and fish oils are useful in helping prevent heart disease. Olive oil contains high concentrations of fatty acids with one carbon–carbon double bond (known as mono-unsaturated fatty acids), and fish oils contain high concentrations of fatty acids with more than one carbon–carbon double bond (known as polyunsaturated fatty acids). The link between unsaturated fatty acids and health has led to a variety of food products being advertised as 'healthy', based on their unsaturated fat content (*figure 5.23*).

Food constituent	Available energy ($kJ\,g^{-1}$ dry weight)
fat	37
carbohydrate	17
protein	17

● **Table 5.3** The available energy content of the major food constituents.

Triglycerides, and the long-chain fatty acids stored in them, are not only important as energy stores. They are also used to synthesise other important molecules. Therefore, their availability is important for the body to function properly. Most long-chain fatty acids can be synthesised by animal cells. However, two essential fatty acids must be obtained from our diet. One of these is linoleic acid, which is the starting material for many vital compounds including some of the phosphoglycerides used to make cell membranes.

● **Figure 5.23** The claim that some foods are 'healthy' is based on the amount and type of fat content.

Other roles of lipids

In addition to providing an energy store and material for cell membranes, fat tissue under the skin and around vital organs provides the body with heat insulation and some protection from injury.

SAQ 5.4

Lipids, fatty acids and carbohydrates are all energy sources.

The enthalpy change for the complete combustion of octadecanoic acid is $-40\,kJ\,g^{-1}$ and that of glucose is $-16\,kJ\,g^{-1}$.

a Copy and complete the following equation for the complete combustion of octadecanoic acid and calculate its enthalpy change of combustion per mole.
$C_{18}H_{36}O_2 +$ _____ $\rightarrow$ _____ + _____ ($\Delta H =$ _____ $kJ\,mol^{-1}$)
M_r(octadecanoic acid) $= 284$

b Suggest why lipids and fatty acids have a higher energy content than glucose and other carbohydrates.

c Suggest two reasons why animals tend to store energy in the form of fat rather than carbohydrate.

SUMMARY

- Lipids are a class of structurally diverse biological compounds that are grouped together on the basis of their solubility. Due to their weakly polar nature, lipids are insoluble in water and soluble in organic solvents.

- Triglycerides are esters formed from long-chain carboxylic acids and propan-1,2,3-triol (glycerol). They occur in animal fats and vegetable oils.

- The long, unbranched hydrocarbon chains of the carboxylic acid components of triglycerides results in these molecules being soluble in non-polar solvents and not in water.

- Phosphoglycerides are the major lipid component of cell membranes.

- Phosphoglyceride molecules consist of two distinct regions: a polar 'head' and a non-polar 'tail'.

- Treatment of suspensions of phosphoglycerides in water results in the formation of bimolecular layers.

- Lipids are a concentrated energy store of carbon and hydrogen.

- Carbohydrates serve as a short-term, instant energy source for the body.

- Lipids release more energy per gram than do carbohydrates.

Questions

1 a By means of simple labelled diagrams indicate the structural differences between a triglyceride (fat) molecule and a phosphoglyceride.

b (i) What is the difference between a saturated and an unsaturated fat?

(ii) Olive oil is said to be 'rich in mono-unsaturated fats'. What do you understand by the term 'mono-unsaturated'?

(iii) Elaidic acid (octadec-*trans*-9-enoic acid) and oleic acid can be represented by the structural formulae shown below:

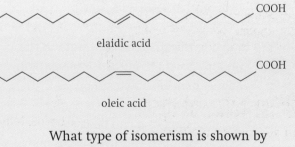

elaidic acid

oleic acid

What type of isomerism is shown by these two fatty acids? What is the systematic name for oleic acid?

2 Shown below is the formula for a saturated fat (a triglyceride).

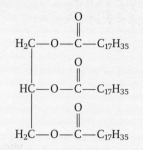

$$H_2C-O-\overset{\displaystyle O}{\overset{\displaystyle \|}{C}}-C_{17}H_{35}$$

a Explain why this fat can be described as saturated. Suggest a chemical test to distinguish between an unsaturated and a saturated fat.

b Give the formulae of the two molecules that have reacted together to form the fat shown.

c On boiling the fat with a concentrated solution of sodium hydroxide, a solid separates out after several minutes.

  (i) Explain what has happened to the fat.

  (ii) Write an equation for this reaction.

  (iii) Give a commercial application for this reaction.

3 a Write a balanced equation for the formation of a fat molecule from propan-1,2,3-triol and palmitic acid ($C_{15}H_{31}COOH$). Your equation should include the structural formula of the organic product, but the long carbon chains may be drawn simply as $C_{15}H_{31}$.

  b (i) Fat can be hydrolysed. Suggest two reagents that can be used to accomplish this hydrolysis, one of which should be an enzyme. Give conditions that are appropriate for each.

  (ii) The carboxylic acid isolated from a hydrolysed fat is non-cyclic and has the molecular formula $C_{17}H_{33}COOH$. Draw one possible chemical structure for this molecule.

  (iii) Describe and explain a chemical test that would distinguish between the fat that is an ester of $C_{15}H_{31}COOH$ and one that is an ester of the carboxylic acid in **b**(ii).

4 a What distinctive features of phospholipid molecules enable them to fulfil their role as a major component of cell membranes?

  b The diagram below represents the structure of a cell membrane.

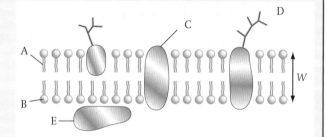

  (i) What term is applied to this model of plasma membrane structure?

  (ii) State the names of components A–E.

  (iii) Give an approximate figure for the width (W) of the plasma membrane.

  (iv) What role does cholesterol play in plasma membranes.

CHAPTER 6

Nucleic acids and protein synthesis

By the end of this chapter you should be able to:

1 describe, in simple terms, the structure of *nucleotides* and their condensation polymers, nucleic acids;

2 describe the chemical and physical differences between DNA and RNA molecules including: the concept of *base pairing*, the part played by *hydrogen bonding*, their *molecular size*, and the *double helix* in DNA compared to single-stranded RNA;

3 explain the role of DNA in the *replication* of genetic information, and in coding for mRNA in the transcription phase of protein synthesis;

4 describe the roles of mRNA and tRNA in the *translation* phase of protein synthesis.

DNA – the source of heredity

Deoxyribonucleic acid (DNA) was discovered in 1869, 10 years after the publication of Darwin's *The Origin of Species*. The Swiss biochemist Friedrich Meischer isolated a sample of DNA from white blood cells in pus sticking to discarded bandages. At this time there was no suspicion of the immense significance of the molecule as the 'vehicle' of heredity and evolution. Not until 1944 did Oswald Avery demonstrate that DNA was the material that transferred genetic information from one cell to another.

A one-page letter published on April 25th 1953 in the scientific journal *Nature* started the recent rapid increase in information about the origins of life, evolutionary development and the transfer of genetic information:

'We wish to suggest a structure for the salt of deoxyribonucleic acid (DNA). This structure has features which are of considerable scientific interest... It has not escaped our notice that the specific base pairing [inherent in the proposed structure] suggests a possible copying mechanism for the genetic material.'

The structure of DNA proposed thus by James Watson and Francis Crick led to the advent of molecular biology and genetic engineering. It was arguably the most important scientific development of the twentieth century. In making their discovery, Watson and Crick used a model-building approach (*figure 6.1*). They based their models on the chemical

● **Figure 6.1** Francis Crick (right) adjusting the model of DNA that he made with James Watson. In the background you can see a sketch of the double helix and a pentagon, representing a deoxyribose, can be seen in the model near Watson's chin.

composition of DNA and, most importantly, on data from X-ray crystallography.

The development of science often builds on previous results. Elucidating the structure of DNA would have been impossible without the discovery of X-rays in 1895. Then in 1925, von Laue showed that the diffraction of X-rays could be used to find the arrangement of atoms in crystals. The method was successfully applied to determine the structure of proteins, including myoglobin and insulin, for example. Then, in 1952, Rosalind Franklin, working with Maurice Wilkins, shone X-rays onto crystalline forms of DNA and produced diffraction patterns that were both beautiful and complex (*figure 6.2*).

The ordered X-ray patterns produced reflected the regularity of a double helical structure. Two DNA strands, running in opposite directions, are linked together in a ladder-like molecule – but a twisted ladder, a right-handed helix (*figure 6.3*). Each DNA strand is a condensation polymer of sugar molecules and phosphate groups. Attached to this sugar–phosphate backbone is a sequence of organic bases constructed from a choice of just four, often referred to simply by the first letter of their names: A, C, G and T. Heredity information is stored as the sequence of these bases along the chain. The genetic message is written in a language of only four letters.

Since the publication of the structure of DNA in 1953, there has been a dramatic increase in the amount of information and technology available for research. This has generated some of the most amazing opportunities for understanding but also raised some of the gravest ethical questions. Our

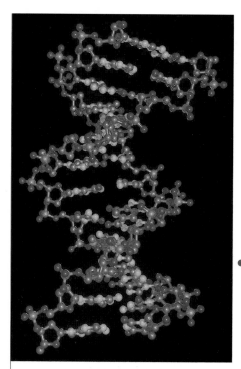

● **Figure 6.3** A computer-generated model of DNA, showing the right-handed double helix.

understanding and ability to manipulate genetic material has led, for instance, to possibilities for gene therapy in a range of health disorders, genetic modification of crops, and the production of medically useful antibodies and proteins in cloned animals. One major breakthrough, in 2001, was the completion of the 'map' of the entire human genome (all the DNA in a cell). As scientists explore how this information can be used, the significance of this immense project can only increase.

The structures of DNA and RNA

Deoxyribonucleic acid (DNA) and ribonucleic acid (RNA) are essential components of all living cells. They are involved in the transmission of heredity information and in the production of the vast range of proteins made by cells. Both molecules are synthesised in cells by the condensation polymerisation of nucleotides (see later). Both DNA and RNA are polynucleotides. Their structures are similar although, as their names suggest, not identical.

DNA controls heredity on a molecular level:

■ it is a self-replicating molecule capable of passing genetic information from one generation to the next;

■ it contains in its base sequence the genetic code used to synthesise proteins.

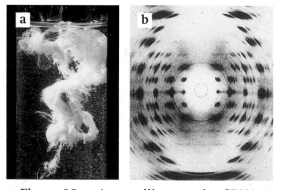

● **Figure 6.2** **a** A crystalline sample of DNA. A sample such as this would have been used by Rosalind Franklin to produce the X-ray diffraction photograph shown in **b**.

Various forms of RNA are involved in the processes of 'gene expression' that result in the production of proteins.

Building DNA

DNA is built up from units called **nucleotides**. Each strand of DNA is made by the condensation polymerisation of these monomer nucleotides. Nucleotides are themselves made from three components (*figure 6.4*):

■ a sugar;
■ a phosphate group;
■ a nitrogen-containing organic base.

The sugar molecule in the nucleotides that make up DNA is deoxyribose, a pentose (see chapter 4).

The phosphate group is attached to deoxyribose by an ester link with the hydroxyl group (−OH) on the 5' carbon of the sugar (the numbering of the carbon atoms in nucleotides is explained below).

The final components of the nucleotides in DNA are the nitrogen-containing bases. There are four different bases, all of which are cyclic compounds formed of carbon, nitrogen and hydrogen (*figure 6.5*):

■ adenine (A);
■ guanine (G);
■ thymine (T);
■ cytosine (C).

Two of the bases, adenine (A) and guanine (G), are purines. They both have a planar two-ring structure. The other two bases, thymine (T) and cytosine (C), are pyrimidines and have a planar single-ring structure.

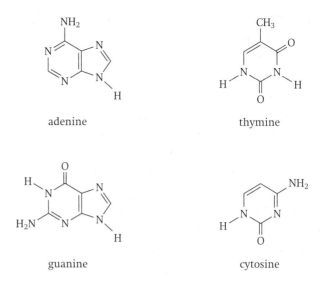

● **Figure 6.5** The four bases used in DNA.

SAQ 6.1

The diagram below represents the basic chemical unit from which the nucleic acid DNA is formed.

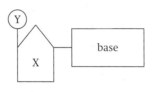

a State the name of:
  (i) the whole chemical unit shown;
  (ii) the component labelled X;
  (iii) the component labelled Y.
b (i) Name two nitrogenous bases present in DNA, one a purine and the other a pyrimidine.
  (ii) Suggest the most appropriate name for each of the following outline structures: purine or pyrimidine.

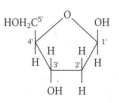

I   II

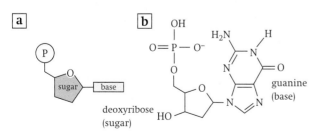

● **Figure 6.4 a** The three components that make up a nucleotide. **b** The nucleotide made up from phosphate, deoxyribose and guanine.

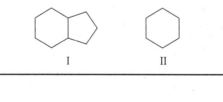

● **Figure 6.6** The numbering of deoxyribose in DNA. Note the use of ' (prime) and that the atoms are numbered clockwise.

The numbering of the atoms in the ring structures of a nucleotide becomes significant when describing DNA. The atoms in the bases are given plain numbers and so the carbon atoms in deoxyribose are numbered from 1′ to 5′ (spoken as 'one-prime' and 'five-prime') (*figure 6.6*).

In building a DNA strand, the phosphate group on the 5′ carbon of one nucleotide reacts with the –OH group of the 3′ carbon of the next nucleotide. The reaction is a condensation reaction in which water is eliminated – an ester link is formed. A strand of DNA is therefore a linear condensation polymer. Whereas the backbone of a protein molecule is a polypeptide chain (see chapter 2), the backbone of a strand of nucleic acid is a polyester chain (*figure 6.7*).

In DNA, ester links are formed between sugar molecules (which contain –OH groups) and phosphoric acid groups. (An ester is a compound formed in a condensation reaction between an alcohol and an acid – esters are discussed in *Chemistry 2*, chapter 4.)

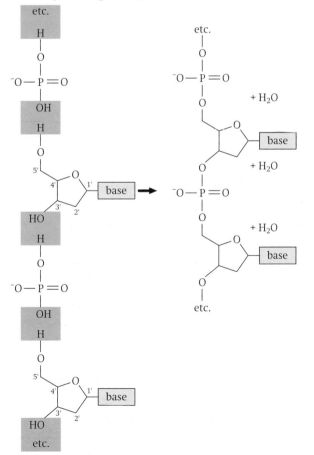

● **Figure 6.7** The sugar–phosphate backbone of DNA is formed by condensation reactions that produce a polyester.

Box 6A DNA discoveries

In 1950 Erwin Chargaff analysed the base content of DNA from different species of organism using paper chromatography (*table 6.1*). His results showed the intriguing finding that, although the proportions of the bases varied between species, the number of purines equalled the number of pyrimidines in any sample of DNA.

Chargaff went on to show that the DNA from any tissue of a particular species has equal numbers of adenine and thymine residues and equal numbers of guanine and cytosine residues. Watson and Crick realised that this evidence was crucial and used it, together with the X-ray crystallography data collected by Rosalind Franklin and Maurice Wilkins, in proposing their model of the DNA double helix.

Source of DNA	Adenine, A (molar %)	Thymine, T (molar %)	Cytosine, C (molar %)	Guanine, G (molar %)
bacteria	15.1	14.6	35.4	34.9
wheat	27.3	27.1	22.8	22.7
salmon	29.7	29.1	20.4	20.8
human	30.9	29.4	19.8	19.9

● **Table 6.1** The molar proportions of A, T, C and G in samples of DNA.

Building RNA

The nucleotides in RNA are also formed from a sugar, a phosphate group and a nitrogen-containing base.

■ In RNA the sugar is ribose (*figure 6.8* and chapter 4).

■ In an RNA molecule the phosphate group is again attached to the 5′ carbon of the sugar.

■ RNA contains four nitrogen-containing bases: adenine (A), guanine (G), *uracil* (U) (*figure 6.8*) and cytosine (C). In RNA uracil replaces thymine.

RNA is again a condensation polymer in which the phosphate group links the 5′ carbon of one nucleotide with the 3′ carbon atom of the next.

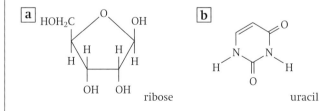

● **Figure 6.8** A strand of RNA is very similar to a strand of DNA. The differences are **a** ribose in RNA (rather than deoxyribose in DNA) and **b** uracil in RNA (rather than thymine in DNA).

DNA in detail

A DNA molecule consists of two strands. Each strand of DNA is a condensation polymer of sugar molecules and phosphate groups, that forms a sugar–phosphate backbone (see *figure 6.7*). The phosphate group links the 5′ carbon atom of one nucleotide with the 3′ carbon atom of the next. The phosphate group is involved in two ester bonds with −OH groups on the sugars. This linkage is referred to as a phosphodiester link.

Attached to this sugar–phosphate backbone is a sequence of nitrogen-containing bases, chosen from the four alternatives shown in *figure 6.5*. It is the sequence of these bases along the sugar–phosphate backbone that stores heredity information.

The two strands in a molecule of DNA are twisted together in a double helix. The nitrogen-containing bases in each DNA strand are positioned between the two sugar–phosphate chains. The bases lie at right angles to the backbone, filling the space between the strands. The bases only fit between the sugar–phosphate chains if a large two-ring structure (a purine: adenine or guanine) is paired with a small single ring structure (a pyrimidine: thymine or cytosine).

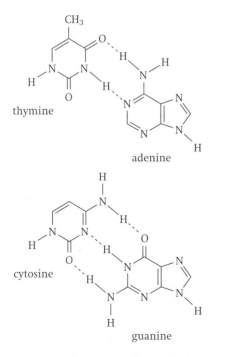

● **Figure 6.9** Complementary base pairing between the bases in DNA. Thymine pairs with adenine by two hydrogen bonds and cytosine pairs with guanine by three hydrogen bonds.

The bases in each pair interact with each other through hydrogen bonding, in the following ways:
■ adenine is always paired with thymine;
■ guanine is always paired with cytosine.
This is known as **complementary base pairing** (*figure 6.9*, and see also *Box 6A*). Note that two hydrogen bonds form between each adenine–thymine pair (A⋯T) and three hydrogen bonds form between each guanine–cytosine pair (G⋯C).

This difference in the hydrogen bonding between the pairs, together with the size considerations (two-ring structures and single-ring structures), ensures the complementary base pairing seen in DNA.

SAQ 6.2

The following diagram indicates the complementary base pairing which occurs in the double helix of the DNA molecule. The sugar is deoxyribose.

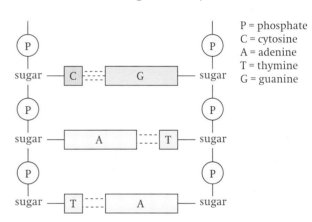

P = phosphate
C = cytosine
A = adenine
T = thymine
G = guanine

a What type of bonding holds the two chains of the double helix together?
b (i) Why is the base pairing described as complementary?
  (ii) Why do other base pairs almost never occur?

The planar nitrogen-containing bases in each strand of DNA are stacked one above each other. Hydrogen bonds between base pairs hold two DNA chains together. Instantaneous dipole-induced dipole attractions between stacks of bases produce the helical structure (*figures 6.10* and *6.11*).

Each DNA strand has a 'direction'. There will be a 'free' 5′ carbon atom at one end and a 'free' 3′ carbon atom at the other. The two DNA strands that make up a DNA molecule run in opposite directions – they are anti-parallel.

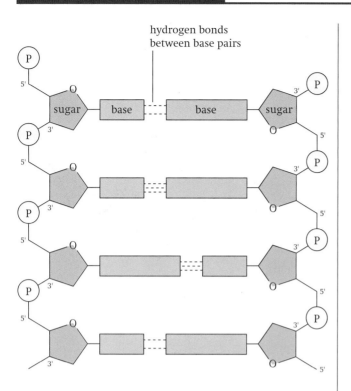

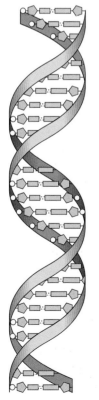

● **Figure 6.10** The formation of the DNA double helix. It is stabilised by hydrogen bonds between the base pairs. Note the two strands run in different directions.

● **Figure 6.11** The double helix formed from two DNA strands. The sugar–phosphate backbone is on the outside and the bases are in the centre. Instantaneous dipole-induced dipole forces maintain the helical structure. Without such forces DNA would be a 'ladder' rather than a double helix.

These two strands are coiled round each other, with the bases on the inside and the sugar–phosphate backbone on the outside (*figure 6.11*).

SAQ 6.3

a Representing molecules of purine or pyrimidine bases by **B**, sugars by **S** and phosphoric acid or phosphate groups by **P**, and using no other symbols, draw a diagram to show how these are linked in a short length of double-stranded DNA. Use full lines (__) for normal covalent bonds and dotted lines (.....) for hydrogen bonds.

b Your sketch makes the two strands look identical. Ignoring the difference between the bases:
  (i) explain how the two strands differ;
  (ii) give the technical term which describes this difference;
  (iii) state how it is indicated on diagrams of DNA.

c When a DNA molecule is gently heated in solution, the two chains gradually separate. The temperature at which 50% of the helical structure is lost is called the melting temperature. Explain why the melting temperature of a particular DNA sequence is dependent upon the percentage of [GC] base pairs in the DNA.

RNA in detail

The individual strands of RNA are very similar to DNA strands in that they both contain a sugar–phosphate backbone, with nitrogen-containing bases attached to the sugar molecules. RNA molecules are polynucleotides containing ribose as the sugar component rather than deoxyribose. This is the first major difference between RNA and DNA.

The second major difference between RNA and DNA is that the base uracil (U) replaces thymine in the set of four bases used to build the polymer. Like thymine, uracil is a pyrimidine and can form a complementary base pair with adenine (*figure 6.12*).

The third major difference between RNA and DNA is that DNA molecules are double-stranded and RNA molecules are single-stranded.

The structures of RNA and DNA are compared in *table 6.2*.

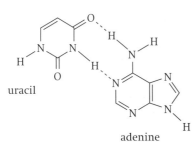

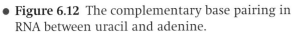

- **Figure 6.12** The complementary base pairing in RNA between uracil and adenine.

Although an RNA molecule is a single long chain, it can bend back on itself to form hairpin loops that are held together by hydrogen bonds between complementary purine and pyrimidine bases. Such loops are important features of the structures of rRNA and tRNA molecules (see page 78). For example, the cloverleaf folding of tRNA molecules enables them to carry out their important function in protein synthesis (*figure 6.13*).

Role of DNA – chains of information

The astounding and compelling neatness of the structure of DNA is that it contains a built-in mechanism for information transfer. DNA strands are capable of self-recognition and self-replication. Duplication of the genetic information takes place every time a cell divides. This means that information encoded in the structure can be passed from one generation to another. Parent DNA molecules can replicate to produce identical daughter copies.

The structure of DNA is also used in nature to store the blueprint for the synthesis of proteins.

Factor	Deoxyribonucleic acid	Ribonucleic acid
sugar	pentose sugar is deoxyribose	pentose sugar is ribose
bases	<ul><li>adenine</li><li>cytosine</li><li>guanine</li><li>thymine</li></ul>	<ul><li>adenine</li><li>cytosine</li><li>guanine</li><li>uracil</li></ul>
structure	double helix of two anti-parallel strands	single-stranded, though the chain can fold on itself to form helical loops

- **Table 6.2** Comparison of the structures of DNA and RNA.

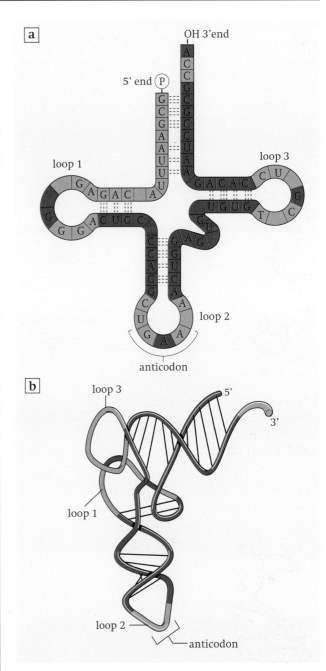

- **Figure 6.13** RNA, although single-stranded, can form helical loops by bending back on itself. Here, tRNA has a 'cloverleaf'-type structure with four sections containing base-paired regions. The role of tRNA in protein synthesis is explained on page 78.

Broadly speaking, the amino acid sequence of each polypeptide chain is encoded in a specific stretch of DNA (a gene). The code in a gene is used to make copies of a particular polypeptide chain through a two-stage process.

- Transcription: the DNA template is first copied (transcribed) into an intermediate nucleic acid molecule, messenger ribonucleic acid (mRNA).

■ Translation: mRNA molecules programme the assembly of the polypeptide chain, involving ribosomes attaching to, and moving along, the mRNA as the protein chain is synthesised.

Thus DNA, by the processes of transcription and translation, is ultimately responsible for the structure of all the proteins synthesised by cells.

So, to reiterate, DNA both preserves the genetic information (replication), and directs the synthesis of proteins (transcription and translation). This is sometimes referred to as the 'central dogma of molecular biology'.

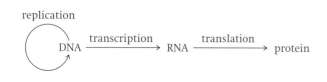

DNA molecules are enormous macromolecules. They need to be, as the DNA contains the essential genetic information that defines the organism concerned. The molecular sizes increase with the complexity of the organism:

■ the DNA of a bacterial virus (bacteriophage λ) shown in *figure 6.14a* is 166 000 base pairs (166 kilobases) in length;

■ the DNA of the bacterium *E. coli* contains about 4 700 000 base pairs (4700 kilobases) (*figure 6.14b*);

■ in animal cells the DNA is packaged into chromosomes, which are each thought to consist of a single molecule of DNA with associated proteins;

■ the length of DNA in each of the human chromosomes varies from 48 000 000 to 240 000 000 base pairs (48 000 to 240 000 kilobases) (*figure 6.14c*).

The folding of such lengths of DNA into the compact chromosomes that become visible under a light microscope at cell division represents an amazing feat of packaging. It also emphasises the enormity of the problem tackled by the Human Genome Project in mapping human DNA. Another point to note is that only a small proportion of all of this DNA codes for proteins. The remainder is a mixture of 'junk' and sections that regulate the decoding itself. The functional regions of DNA are known as genes.

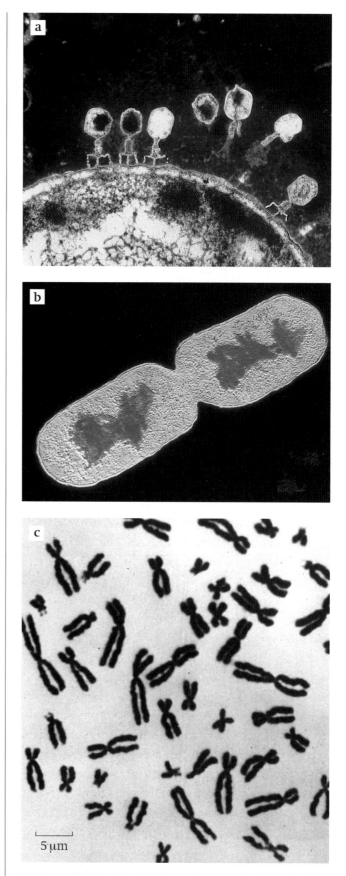

5 μm

● **Figure 6.14 a** An electronmicrograph of bacterial viruses (× 83 000) with the viral DNA visible; **b** an electronmicrograph of the DNA of the bacterium *E.coli*; **c** a photograph of human chromosomes.

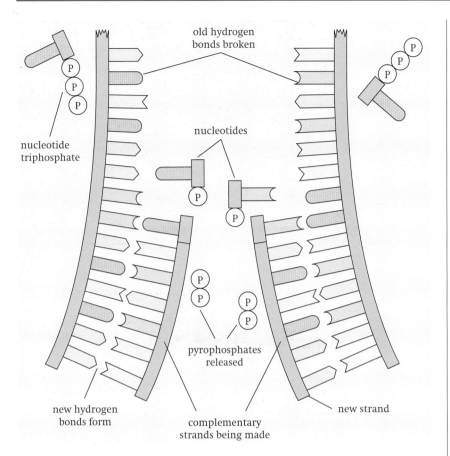

● **Figure 6.15** The process of DNA replication.

Replication – biological assembly of new DNA

The process of formation of new DNA molecules is catalysed by the enzyme DNA polymerase. The new nucleotide units are fed into the reaction process in the form of nucleotide triphosphates (*figure 6.15*). The breakdown of the triphosphate to the monophosphate liberates an inorganic pyrophosphate. The pyrophosphate is then hydrolysed. This exothermic reaction provides the energy for the addition of the next nucleic acid residue.

During replication, the hydrogen bonds and instantaneous dipole-induced dipole forces between the base pairs in the double helix are broken. The original strands act as templates for the synthesis of two new strands. Each new strand contains a sequence of bases complementary to the bases of the original strand.

Hydrogen bonds and van der Waals' forces form between the original and new strands, creating a stable helical structure. Thus, two daughter molecules are formed from the parent double helix (*figure 6.16*). This form of replication is known as semi-conservative replication, because each daughter molecule contains one newly produced strand and one strand from the original DNA molecule.

Since the nucleotides in DNA differ only in the bases they carry, the sequence of the monomers in a DNA strand can be recorded simply as the base sequence. Each nucleotide can be thought of as a single letter in an alphabet that consists of only four letters

– A, T, G and C. The sequence of a DNA strand is written from the 5′ to the 3′ end: for example, 5′-GCAGGATTCC.....GT-3′.

The DNA in almost every cell in our bodies should be an identical copy of the DNA in the original fertilised egg. The only exceptions are certain white blood cells and sex cells. Replication is a complex process and crucially errors

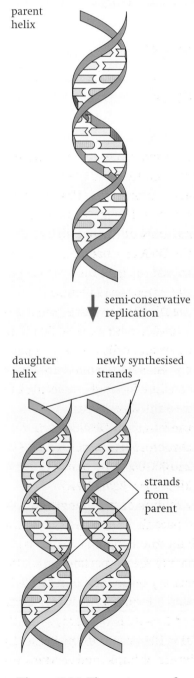

● **Figure 6.16** The outcome of semi-conservative replication.

(mutations) are rare – a remarkable average of only one incorrect base per cell division. Such mutations can be lethal. For example, if they were to occur in a gene involved in deciding whether a cell should divide or not, they might cause uncontrolled cell division and thence cancer. Fortunately, as genes make up only a small percentage of DNA, most mutations are harmless.

SAQ 6.4

a What role do hydrogen bonds play in the accurate replication of DNA?

b DNA is replicated semi-conservatively. What is meant by this term?

c (i) What type of interaction takes place between the bases in the two DNA strands?

(ii) Condensation reactions are involved in the formation of DNA. What is the name given to the links which form the backbone of a DNA strand?

Expressing the message

The roles of RNA

The genetic message encoded in the DNA of cells is used to form protein molecules by the processes of transcription and translation. These two processes together are termed gene expression, and involve several different types of ribonucleic acid (RNA) molecules, each with a different role.

■ Messenger RNA (mRNA) – this is made by copying the DNA gene sequence for a particular polypeptide chain. The message encoded in the mRNA molecule is translated into the primary sequence of a polypeptide chain.

■ Transfer RNA (tRNA) – these molecules transport amino acids to ribosomes for protein synthesis. Each

tRNA recognises the coding sequence for a particular amino acid in mRNA. tRNA molecules are about 75 nucleotides long and represent up to 15% of cellular RNA.

■ Ribosomal RNA (rRNA) – ribosomes are the sites of protein synthesis within cells. A number of different rRNA molecules form part of the structure of ribosomes and account for up to 80% of the RNA within a cell. The larger molecules contain over 3500 nucleotides.

SAQ 6.5

State three ways in which the structure of DNA differs from that of RNA.

Delivering the message

Transcription

Genes contain unique sequences of the four nucleotide bases and so code for different polypeptide chains. The gene sequences are always written in the 5′ → 3′ direction. The gene for a particular polypeptide chain is not copied directly into an amino acid sequence. The code is first transcribed to a molecule of mRNA by the enzyme RNA polymerase. Part of the DNA double helix

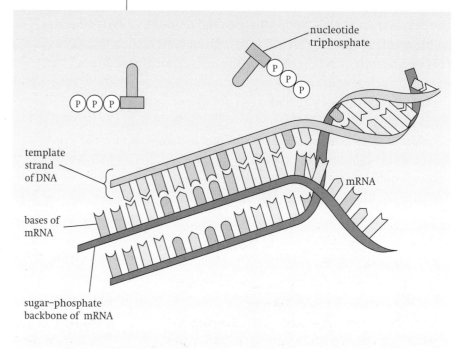

● **Figure 6.17** The process of transcription.

unravels and an RNA copy of the gene is synthesised using the appropriate nucleotides (*figure 6.17*). The mRNA molecule is synthesised from the 5′ end to the 3′ end. (This is also the direction in which the message will subsequently be translated on the ribosomes.)

SAQ 6.6

The following diagram represents part of a DNA molecule and an mRNA molecule.

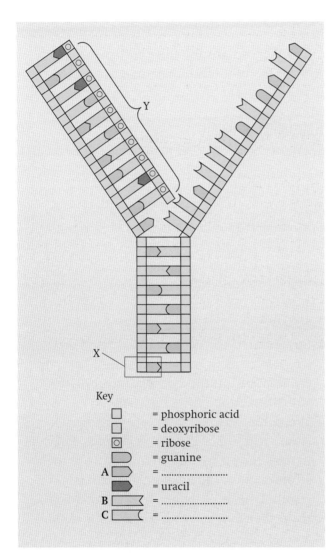

Key

▢	= phosphoric acid
▢	= deoxyribose
◉	= ribose
▭	= guanine
A ▭	= ....
▰	= uracil
B ▭	= ....
C ▭	= ....

a Name molecules A, B and C left blank in the key.

b (i) What is the name given to the molecular sub-unit shown in the box X?

   (ii) Give the names of the component molecules which make up this structure.

c Give two pieces of evidence from the diagram which indicate that the molecule Y is RNA and not half a strand of DNA.

Translation

Ribosomes are the cellular 'machines' that synthesise protein chains. They complete the fascinating sequence of events by which the genetically encoded message is used to synthesise proteins.

During translation several ribosomes attach to a particular mRNA molecule at one time. As the ribosomes move along the mRNA the sequence of bases directs the bringing together of amino acids in the correct order to produce proteins. The language of transcribed RNA, the order of the bases along the mRNA, is translated into the language of proteins, the order of amino acids along a polypeptide chain. tRNA is used as a 'carrier' molecule, as will be seen later.

The genetic code

DNA and mRNA molecules each contain only four nitrogen-containing bases, but there are 20 amino acids used to make proteins. Therefore, the unique sequence of amino acids in a polypeptide chain must be coded for by groups of bases.

If the bases in mRNA were taken two at a time – AA, AC, AG, AU, CA, CC, etc. – only 16 combinations (4^2) would be possible. A three-base (triplet) code provides 64 possible combinations (4^3).

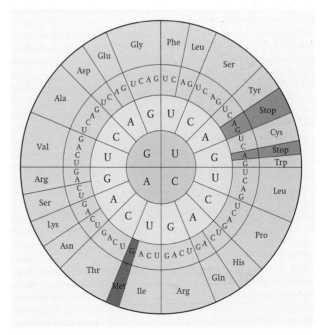

● **Figure 6.18** Codons for amino acids. Codons are read from the 5′ end to the 3′ end on mRNA. On this diagram, this is shown from the centre outwards.

This would allow coding for 64 different amino acids if each triplet coded for just one amino acid. Biochemical and genetic evidence has established that the information in mRNA is a comma-less, non-overlapping triplet code. The message is read from the 5′ end of the mRNA to the 3′ end. Each triplet of bases is referred to as a codon.

The complete genetic code is shown in *figure 6.18*. Interestingly, most amino acids are coded for by more than one triplet combination. Indeed, some amino acids (e.g. arginine) have as many as six possible codons. For all amino acids except methionine and tryptophan, more than one base is allowed in the third position of the codon. This offers some protection from mutations since a base change in the third position of a codon will often result in the codon still coding for the same amino acid residue.

SAQ 6.7

a Use the table of RNA codons below to work out the base sequence in the mRNA fragment which would code for the peptide Pro–Val–Glu,

RNA codon	Amino acid
GUA	valine (Val)
CCU	proline (Pro)
GAA	glutamic acid (Glu)

indicating the 5′ end.

b Write down the base sequence for the DNA fragment from which the mRNA would have been transcribed, again indicating the 5′ end.

c Re-draw your DNA strand and write beside it the complementary strand, again labelling the 5′ end in each strand.

d Draw the double–stranded DNA fragment which would lead, via transcription and translation, to the tripeptide Pro–Glu–Glu.

e Usually only one strand of double helical DNA is used to direct synthesis of a given protein. Suggest why the complementary strand cannot be used.

Starting and stopping translation

All polypeptide chains have a defined length and sequence. For this reason there must be a codon for the first amino acid in the chain (the amino-terminal end) and one to stop the addition of further residues. The 'start' signal is 5′-AUG-3′, which codes for methionine. The 'start' signal ensures that the series of triplet codons that follow is read in the correct groups of three. Consequently the first amino acid in any newly synthesised chain is always methionine. However, in many cases it is removed after translation is complete. There are also three codons that do not code for an amino acid. These codons act as 'stop' signals to end the assembly of a polypeptide chain.

Translation in detail

Amino acids cannot bind to mRNA. tRNA molecules act as the vehicles for these interactions. One end of a tRNA molecule can bind to a specific amino acid. At the other end it has a specific triplet of bases (anticodon) that can bind to the codon on mRNA. Each tRNA, carrying its specific amino acid, can interact with the ribosome and the correct codon on the messenger RNA to begin translation. The translation process is a complex one involving three steps: initiation, elongation and termination.

- Initiation: methionine tRNA, carrying the amino acid methionine, recognises the 'start' codon in the mRNA sequence (AUG) via the anticodon on the tRNA molecule.
- Elongation: a second tRNA, carrying the next amino acid, attaches to the next codon. Enzymes transfer the methionine from its tRNA to the second amino acid, linking them through a peptide bond (see chapter 2). As the ribosome moves along the mRNA sequence, new amino acids are brought to the site of chain elongation by tRNA. Each time the growing polypeptide chain is attached to the new amino acid and the chain grows from the amino-terminal to the carboxy-terminal end (*figure 6.19*).
- Termination: when a 'stop' codon is reached, the complete protein chain is released.

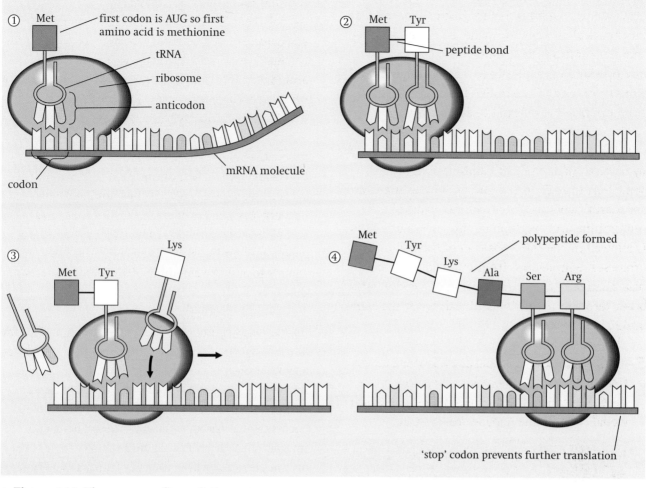

● **Figure 6.19** The process of translation.

SAQ 6.8 _____

a Outline the roles of the several kinds of RNA in the biosynthesis of proteins.

b The peptide fragment
–Tyr–Ser–Ala–Ala–Glu–Gly–Ala–Val–
is known to be coded somewhere inside the fragment of mRNA below. *The start of this fragment may not coincide with the start of a codon.*
5′-GUUACUCUGCUGCUGAAGGAGCUGUAC-3′
Use the above information to work out the codons for alanine and tyrosine.

c Give the base sequence matching the codon for tyrosine in the DNA from which the RNA was transcribed, indicating the direction of the bases in the DNA strand.

SUMMARY

- There are two forms of nucleic acid: one is DNA (deoxyribonucleic acid), in which the sugar is deoxyribose; the other is RNA (ribonucleic acid), where the sugar is ribose.

- Nucleotides are the monomeric units from which the nucleic acids are built. The nucleotides themselves are made from a sugar, a nitrogen-containing base and a phosphate group.

- Both forms of nucleic acid are linear condensation polymers in which the sugar–phosphate backbone of the chain is linked by phosphodiester bonds. The 5′-carbon atom of one sugar molecule is linked to the 3′-carbon atom of the next via a phosphate group. The nitrogen-containing bases are attached to this backbone on the 1′-carbon atom of the sugar.

- DNA has a double-stranded structure. The strands are arranged so that the sugar–phosphate backbones are on the outside of the structure, with the bases pointing inwards towards each other. The chains run in opposite directions to each other – they are anti-parallel – and interact with each other through hydrogen bonds between the bases. The double-stranded DNA molecule is twisted on itself into a right-handed double helix held together by instantaneous dipole-induced dipole forces.

- There are four bases in DNA: adenine (A), guanine (G), thymine (T) and cytosine (C). The hydrogen bonding between these bases is quite specific and means that an adenine in one chain always pairs with a thymine in the other strand, while guanine always pairs with cytosine. This type of pairing is known as complementary base pairing.

- RNA differs from DNA in three major ways. As well as the difference in the sugar unit, RNA molecules contain the base uracil rather than thymine and are single-stranded polymers.

- Complementary base pairing is the molecular basis for the process of replication – the production of identical copies of the genetic code from one generation of cells to the next. The process of replication is semi-conservative: after cell division the new DNA molecules consist of one parent strand and one daughter strand.

- DNA carries the genetic code for the production of proteins.

- Using the genetic code to synthesise proteins involves several types of RNA: messenger RNA (mRNA), transfer RNA (tRNA) and ribosomal RNA (rRNA).

- The processes involved in synthesising proteins based on the genetic code in DNA are known as transcription and translation. Each gene codes for a single polypeptide chain. Transcription involves the copying of the gene into an mRNA molecule. This molecule is then translated into the polypeptide chain in a complex process involving the ribosomes of a cell.

- mRNA molecules contain a triplet code in which three bases in the RNA sequence code for one amino acid in the polypeptide chain.

- tRNA brings specific amino acids to the ribosomes and binds to specific codons in the mRNA molecule. Protein synthesis then takes place in three stages: initiation, elongation and termination.

Questions

1 The structure shown below represents a small piece of deoxyribonucleic acid.

```
         3′
SUGAR — G
   |
PHOSPHATE
   |
SUGAR — G
   |
PHOSPHATE
   |
SUGAR — A
   |
PHOSPHATE
   |
SUGAR — T
   |
PHOSPHATE
   |
SUGAR — C
   |
PHOSPHATE
   |
SUGAR — C
         5′
```

A shorthand way of writing this structure is 5′-GGATCC-3′.

a What is the meaning of the labels 5′ and 3′ in these representations of DNA?

b This small piece of DNA is self-complemetary. This means that two molecules of 5′-GGATCC-3′ will form a piece of double-stranded DNA. Draw the structure of this double-stranded piece of DNA. A shorthand version of this structure is acceptable.

c An enzyme converts the terminal phosphate groups of DNA (there is a terminal phosphate group at each end of a DNA strand) into soluble phosphate which can be isolated as insoluble magnesium ammonium phosphate ($MgNH_4PO_4$, M_r = 137). In one experiment on a sample of double-stranded DNA known to be phosphorylated on all its terminal 3′ and 5′ hydroxyl groups, 2.74×10^{-3} g of magnesium ammonium phosphate were formed.

(i) Calculate the number of moles of DNA in the original sample.

(ii) If the mass of DNA originally used was 8.25×10^{-2} g, calculate the relative molecular mass of this sample of DNA.

(iii) The average relative molecular mass of double-stranded DNA, 10 base pairs long, is 6600. Calculate the length of the piece of DNA (in base pairs) used in this experiment.

(iv) If this piece of DNA was found in the middle of a gene, what is the maximum number of amino acids for which it could code?

2 . . . . .AGAAGAGAAGCU . . . .

The above sequence of bases is part of a nucleic acid.

a (i) What information is missing from the above which enables the full structural formula to be drawn unambiguously?

(ii) Is the nucleic acid DNA or RNA? Explain your answer.

(iii) Give the name of one purine and one pyrimidine.

b When the complete sequence (of which the above 12 bases are a tiny part) is expressed, the hormone insulin is synthesised.

(i) What kind of compound is insulin?

(ii) Apart from the possibility of translating sequences of bases into molecules of the wrong length, there is another important reason why there must be a 'start' codon somewhere in the sequence. What is this reason?

3　The following abbreviations are used in diagrams of nucleic acids:

P = phosphate; A = adenine; C = cytosine; S = sugar; U = uracil; G = guanine

a　Use these abbreviations to draw a simple block diagram of the structure of DNA, showing three different nucleotides.

b　The base sequence of DNA for a specific tetrapeptide is:
CGACATGAACCG

　(i)　Write down the base sequence of the mRNA transcribed from the above DNA sequence.

　(ii)　Given the following mRNA triplet codes, deduce the amino acid sequence of the tetrapeptide.

Alanine	GCU
Aspartic acid	GAU
Glycine	GGC or GGA
Leucine	CUU
Valine	GUA
Isoleucine	AUU

　(iii)　If a mutation occurs in which all three G bases in the DNA are converted into T bases, deduce the amino acid sequence in the mutant tetrapeptide.

c　(i)　Explain why the changing of a base in a codon may still result in it coding for the same amino acid.

　(ii)　Explain how the synthesis of a polypeptide chain is terminated.

4　Mutation of the mRNA of a T4 bacteriophage (a virus) leads to the omission of one base at the beginning of a sequence of 15 bases so that the rest are displaced by one position in the 5′ direction, as shown below.

Normal　5′- AGUCCAUCACUUAAU - 3′
Mutant　5′- GUCCAUCACUUAAUG - 3′

a　Use the genetic code in *figure 6.18* to translate each of these base sequences into amino acid sequences in the normal and mutant proteins.

b　Write down the sequence of bases in the piece of DNA which would produce the normal mRNA sequence after transcription, identifying the 3′ and 5′ ends.

c　How are the base, phosphate and sugar parts of each nucleotide linked in a single strand of DNA?

d　The normal amino acid sequence is part of the enzyme lysozyme. Explain how the mutation might affect the activity of the enzyme; in your answer, refer to the DNA and RNA involved in its biosynthesis.

Answers to self-assessment questions

Chapter 2

2.1
a An amino group, $-NH_2$.
A carboxylic acid group, $-COOH$.
(Draw the structures to show all the bonds, see page 8.)

b Proline; it has a cyclic structure involving the amino group / it has a secondary amino group.

c Glycine, alanine, valine, leucine, isoleucine, phenylalanine, tryptophan, proline, methionine.

d Serine, threonine, tyrosine, cysteine, asparagine, glutamine.

e Aspartic acid, glutamic acid.

2.2
a (i) $R = CH_2COOH$
(ii) At neutral pH the acid group in the side-chain will be ionised, however at high pH the acid group will not be ionised.

b (i) $R = CH_2CH_2CH_2CH_2NH_2$
(ii) At neutral pH the amino group in the side-chain will be positively charged (NH_3^+), but at low pH it will not be ionised.

2.3
a The amino group carries a lone pair of electrons on the N atom.

b It can therefore accept a proton and show the properties of a base.

2.4
a It would be in the zwitterion form at pH 7 – with both an NH_3^+ and COO^- group present (see page 9).

b Net charge = 0 (zero/no charge).

2.5
a In the solid alanine is in the zwitterionic form (see page 9). This means that it has a higher melting point than might be expected as it is an ionic solid – the electrostatic forces holding the lattice together are relatively strong.

b The polar nature of the amino group and the carboxylic acid group mean that the amino acid molecules can interact with water molecules through hydrogen bonding.

2.6
a 2-aminoethanoic acid.

b A chiral C atom must have 4 different groups attached to it – glycine does not have 4 different groups attached to the central C atom.

c Glycine does not show optical isomerism.

2.7
a Condensation polymerisation.

b (i) Three amino acids polymerised together.
(ii) A polymer chain of more than 20 amino acids. (iii) A longer polymer chain of more than 50 amino acids, protein chains can be up to 1000 amino acids long (note that functional protein molecules may consist of more than one chain; haemoglobin, for example).

2.8
a (i) Ring a CONH grouping; an amide group.
(ii) Three (the tetrapeptide is ala-lys-gly-ala).
(iii) The terminal amino group would be uncharged (NH_2), the amino group on the lysine side-chain would be uncharged (NH_2), and the terminal acid group would be charged (COO^-).

2.9
a See figure 2.8 showing the peptide link – bond angles 120° / a planar structure.

b (i) No freedom of rotation about the C–N bond because of delocalised π cloud.
(ii) The structure arranges itself in the trans form to keep the bulky R groups apart.

2.10
a Covalent bonding.

b They are referred to as the N-terminal and C-terminal ends or the amino-terminal and carboxy-terminal ends.

2.11
a See *figure 2.11*.

b Secondary structure.

c α-helix and β-pleated sheet.

2.12
a 0.54 nm.

b 3.6 amino acids per turn.

c 0.54/3.6 = 0.15 nm.

d 360/3.6 = 100° per amino acid.

2.13 **Lysine** – yes, the NH_2 group in the side-chain can participate in hydrogen bonding; **asparagine** – yes, the amide group ($CONH_2$) in the side-chain is polarised and can participate in hydrogen bonding; **valine** – no, valine has a non-polar side-chain which cannot participate in hydrogen bonding; **aspartic acid** – yes, the acid group (COOH) in the side-chain can take part in hydrogen bonding.

2.14 The amino acids are linked together in a polypeptide chain with peptide link regions between the amino acids – hydrogen bonding between the peptide link regions holds the α-helix in position (secondary structure) – the R-groups of the different amino acid residues are pointing out from the helix and can interact with other R-groups to stabilise tertiary structure – **valine** could participate in hydrophobic interactions (van der Waals' forces) with other non-polar groups – **aspartic acid** could participate in hydrogen bonding with other polar groups or in ionic interactions with other charged groups – **cysteine** could form disulphide bridges with other cysteine residues.

Possible diagrams (see *figures 2.14* and *2.15*)

Disulphide bond formation:

|–CH_2SH $HSCH_2$–| → |–CH_2S – SCH_2–|

Ionic interaction:

|–$(CH_2)_4NH_3^+$ $^-OOCCH_2$–|

2.15 **a** Instantaneous dipole-induced dipole forces.
b Hydrogen bonding.
c Ionic interaction.
d Disulphide bridge.
e Cysteine.

2.16 **a** Two; globin α-chains and globin β-chains.
b (i) The haem group; four.
(ii) Iron, +2 (Fe^{2+} ions).

2.17 **a** Increasing the temperature means that the molecules have greater energy – the chains vibrate more and this disrupts the relatively weak forces holding the secondary and tertiary structure in place – protein molecules lose their shape.

b At extremes of pH polarised groups can gain or lose protons thus interfering with hydrogen bonding which is involved in maintaining secondary and tertiary structure – the ionisation of certain R-groups will also be affected resulting in the loss of ionic interactions that may be stabilising tertiary structure.

2.18 **a** At pH 7 the amino groups in the lysine residues will be charged (NH_3^+) and are able to participate in ionic interactions maintaining tertiary structure – at pH 11 these groups will be uncharged and those ionic interactions will no longer be present, thus disrupting the tertiary structure of the protein.

b Heavy metal ions such as Ag^+ disrupt disulphide bridges – they react with cysteine residues, replacing the H atoms in –SH groups and preventing disulphide bond formation.

Chapter 3

3.1 The fastest reaction would be obtained using the enzyme catalase – the reaction has the lowest activation energy under these conditions.

3.2 Enzyme action depends greatly on molecular recognition and shape – the enzyme is the equivalent of the 'lock' into which the substrate fits like the 'key' – the fit is precise and this explains the high degree of specificity of enzymes – the region of the enzyme into which the substrate fits is the active site – once the products have formed they leave the active site of the enzyme.

3.3 See *figure 3.3*.

3.4 **a** The active site has (i) a substrate binding site, and (ii) a catalytic site.
b The binding and catalytic action of the enzyme are very dependent on molecular recognition and shape – the shape of an active site is designed to recognise just one substrate (or type of substrate).

3.5 **a** See *figure 3.4*.
b See *figure 3.6*.

3.6 a Turnover number is a measure of how many 'reactions' an enzyme molecule can catalyse in a given time – the availability of substrate molecules must not limit this so the substrate must be in excess.

b (i) The turnover number would approximately halve.

(ii) As a very approximate rule enzyme activity changes by a factor of 2 for a 10 °C change in temperature.

3.7 a (i) See *figure 3.9*.

(ii) Initially the rate of reaction is directly proportional to the substrate concentration – the reaction is first order – however at a certain point the curve flattens out as all the active sites on the enzyme molecules become occupied – the enzyme molecules are saturated with substrate – the rate of reaction now depends on the rate of detachment of the substrate from the enzyme molecules.

b (i) See *figure 3.11* – the presence of a competitive inhibitor means that the same plateau is reached, but at a higher substrate concentration.

(ii) A competitive inhibitor has a very similar shape to the actual substrate but does not undergo reaction – it attaches to the enzyme active site, blocking it and inhibiting enzyme activity – competitive inhibition can be overcome by addition of more substrate.

c (i) See *figure 3.14* – the activity reaches a lower plateau when the inhibitor is present.

(ii) A non-competitive inhibitor binds to the enzyme at some point other than the active site, altering the shape of the enzyme so that it doesn't catalyse the reaction – attachment of the inhibitor makes the enzyme non-functional and therefore a lower plateau is reached.

3.8 a An enzyme which is bound, or entrapped in, an insoluble support.

b See *figure 3.16*.

c **Economic advantages** – enzyme can easily be re-isolated and re-used / enzyme can be packed in column and used continuously for longer periods.

Technical advantages – enzyme can be removed from reaction mixture reducing end-product inhibition / greater thermal stability of the enzyme means more productive use.

d Immobilised glucose isomerase used in the production of high fructose syrups. Immobilising the enzyme prevents the product inhibiting the enzyme.

e Enzymes function under milder conditions / enzymes are significantly more efficient catalysts / enzymes have a higher specificity which means there are fewer side-products from reactions.

3.9 a (i) A buffer solution is added to maintain and control the pH – resists changes in pH resulting from the addition of small amounts of acid or alkali.

(ii) See *figure 3.6*.

b (i) A protease, a lipase.

(ii) To digest protein and fat stains respectively.

c Enzymes could begin acting on proteins and fats in the skin / 'foreign' protein on the skin could cause an allergic response.

Chapter 4

4.1 a (i) See *figure 4.4*.

(ii) See *figure 4.5*.

(iii) See *figure 4.3* or *4.7*.

b (i) and (iii) are aldehydes; (ii) is a ketone.

c (i) is a pentose; (ii) and (iii) are hexoses.

4.2 a B

b A, C

c C

d A

e B

4.3 a Isomerism.

b There are five –OH groups in the structure, all of which can form hydrogen bonds with water molecules making the molecules very soluble.

c A is α-glucose as the –OH on carbon-1 is on the opposite side of the ring to the –CH$_2$OH group on carbon 5 (see *figure 4.12*).

4.4 a See *figure 4.13*.

b Hydrolysis with dilute hydrochloric acid is non-specific, all types of glycosidic link are hydrolysed.

The enzyme maltase only hydrolyses 1α-4 glycosidic links – the active site is specific for a particular substrate.

$C_{12}H_{22}O_{11} + H_2O \rightarrow 2C_6H_{12}O_6$

4.5   **a** 1α-4 and 1α-6 links.

      b Hydrolysis.

      c α-glucose, see *figure 4.13*.

      d Amylopectin (or glycogen).

      e The monomer is soluble and immediately accessible to chemical reaction so it cannot function as an energy store / the polymer is insoluble and not immediately metabolised, hence it can function as an energy store.

4.6   **Starch** is a storage polymer of glucose consisting of two molecules: amylose – a straight chain polymer in which the glucose monomers are joined by 1α-4 links, and amylopectin – a branched polymer involving 1α-4 and 1α-6 links.

      Cellulose is a structural polysaccharide consisting of glucose monomers joined by 1β-4 links.

      Humans are able to digest starch molecules as they possess digestive enzymes capable of recognising 1α-4 links and hydrolysing them. Humans do not possess enzymes capable of recognising 1β-4 links and so cannot digest cellulose. Cellulose serves as dietary fibre in the human diet.

Chapter 5

5.1   **a** (i) **Lipids** are a class of biological molecules characterised by their insolubility in water and their solubility in organic solvents – they include triglycerides, phospholipids and steroids.

        (ii) A triacylglycerol or triglyceride is a tri- ester formed between a glycerol molecule and three long-chain fatty acid molecules.

        (iii) An unsaturated fatty acid – a fatty acid is a long-chain carboxylic acid – the acid group is at the end of a long hydrocarbon chain and in this case one (or more) of the carbon to carbon bonds is a double bond.

        (iv) A saturated fatty acid is one in which all the carbon to carbon bonds in the hydrocarbon chains are single bonds.

      b (i) $CH_2OOC\ C_{15}H_{31}$
             |
            $CHOOC\ C_{15}H_{31}$
             |
            $CH_2OOC\ C_{15}H_{31}$

        (ii) An ester link.

        (iii) Solid, as it is a saturated triglyceride.

      c (i) $CH_2OOC(CH_2)_{14}CH_3$
             |
            $CHOOC(CH_2)_{16}CH_3$
             |
            $CH_2OOC(CH_2)_7CH=CHCH_2CH=CH(CH_2)_4CH_3$

        (ii) $CH_2OOC(CH_2)_{14}CH_3$
             |
            $CHOOC(CH_2)_{16}CH_3$
             |
            $CH_2OOC(CH_2)_7CH=CHCH_2CH=CH(CH_2)_{14}COONa$
             ↓
        $CH_2(OH)CH(OH)CH_2OH$
        +
        $CH_3(CH_2)_{14}COONa$
        +
        $CH_3(CH_2)_{16}COONa$
        +
        $CH_3(CH_2)_4CH=CHCH_2CH=CH(CH_2)_7COONa$

5.2   **a** (i) Carbon, hydrogen, oxygen (see *figures 5.1* and *5.7*) (ii) carbon, hydrogen, oxygen, phosphorus, nitrogen (see *figures 5.2* and *5.12*).

      b A triglyceride is a tri- ester formed between a glycerol molecule and three long-chain fatty acid molecules.

      A phospolipid is similar to a triglyceride except that one of the fatty acid chains is replaced by a substituted phosphate group (see *figures 5.7* and *5.12*).

5.4   **a** $C_{18}H_{36}O_2 + 26\ O_2 \rightarrow 18\ CO_2 + 18\ H_2O$

      1 mole = 284 g

      so $\Delta H = -(284 \times 40) = -11\,360\ kJ\,mol^{-1}$

      b Lipids have a higher ratio of carbon and hydrogen per molecule / glucose and other carbohydrates have more oxygen within each molecule and are therefore already partially oxidised.

      c Fats store considerably more energy per g and they have other useful functions; insulation and protection of tissues from abrasion, for example.

Chapter 6

6.1 **a** (i) A (deoxyribo) nucleotide.
(ii) Deoxyribose.
(iii) A phosphate group (phosphoric acid).

  b (i) Purines: adenine, guanine / pyrimidines: thymine, cytosine.
(ii) I = purine; II = pyrimidine

6.2 **a** Hydrogen bonding.

  b (i) The pairing is specific, A always pairs with T and G always with C, no other combinations occur.
(ii) The interactions involve a recognition which is specific: there are two hydrogen bonds between A and T, but three hydrogen bonds between G and C (see *figure 6.9*) / there is a specific fit to the pairing so that the base pairs can fit within the helical structure.

6.3 **a**

```
S — B ⋯ B — S
|           |
P           P
|           |
S — B ⋯ B — S
|           |
P           P
```

  b (i) The strands run in opposite directions.
(ii) They are anti-parallel.
(iii) The ends are designated by the numbers 5′ and 3′ – the numbers of the carbon atoms with 'free' –OH groups at the ends of the chains.

  c The pairing of G to C is stronger as it involves three hydrogen bonds between the bases whereas the A to T pairing only involves two hydrogen bonds, so the higher the GC content of a DNA helix the stronger the interactions between the chains and the higher the melting temperature as more energy will be needed to disrupt the helix.

6.4 **a** When the new strand is built on the template of an old strand the incoming nucleotide is selected for its ability to pair with the base in the old strand – so A is always matched with T etc. / hydrogen bonding plays an important role in this recognition as a different number of hydrogen bonds is involved in each pairing.

  b When each double helix is copied the product molecules each contain one 'old' strand and one 'new' strand (see *figure 6.16*).

  c (i) Hydrogen bonding (and van der Waals' forces between the base pairs 'stacked' on top of each other).
(ii) Phosphodiester links.

6.5 DNA has a double-stranded structure (each molecule has four ends) whereas RNA is single-stranded (each molecule only has two ends). DNA contains the sugar deoxyribose whereas RNA uses ribose. DNA contains the base, thymine, whereas RNA uses uracil.

6.6 **a** A = thymine; B = adenine; C = cytosine.

  b (i) A (deoxyribo) nucleotide.
(ii) Deoxyribose, a base, a phosphate group.

  c Y contains ribose and uracil.

6.7 **a** mRNA sequence: 5′–CCUGUAGAA–3′

  b DNA sequence: 3′–GGACATCTT–5′

  c 3′–GGACATCTT–5′
5′–CCTGTAGAA–3′

  d 3′–GGACTTCTT–5′
5′–CCTGAAGAA–3′

  e The 'start' sequence on the DNA would be at the wrong end of the gene for the polypeptide chain and the sequence would be back to front.

6.8 **a** MessengerRNA: carries the genetic message from DNA that determines the sequence of amino acids in a polypeptide chain / three bases code for each amino acid.

   TransferRNA – specific for each amino acid, they carry the amino acids to the ribosomes / anti-codon sequence on each tRNA recognises the triplet codon in the mRNA.

   Ribosomal RNA: part of the structure of the ribosomes.

  b Codon for alanine: GCU
codon for tyrosine: UAC.

  c 5′–GTA–3′ or 3′–ATG–5′

Biological glossary

alleles different varieties of a gene, which code for different versions of the same characteristic.

antibody a protein (immunoglobulin) made by white blood cells in response to antigen; the variable region of the antibody molecule is complementary in shape to its specific antigen.

antigen a substance that is foreign to the body and stimulates an immune response.

cell a structure bounded by a plasma membrane, containing cytoplasm and organelles. Average diameter 30 µm.

chloroplast an organelle found in many plant cells, which contains chlorophyll, and where photosynthesis takes place.

chromosome a coiled thread of DNA and protein, found in the nucleus of cells.

cytoplasm the fluid within cells surrounding the nucleus and organelles.

endoplasmic reticulum a network of membranes in the cytoplasm of cells, where large molecules are built up from small ones.

epithelium a tissue which covers surfaces either inside or outside the body.

eukaryotic cell a cell containing a nucleus and other membrane-bound organelles. Average diameter 40 µm.

excretion the removal of toxic or excess products of metabolism from the body.

extracellular outside cells.

gamete a sex cell, containing only one of each kind of chromosome. Eggs and sperm are haploid.

gene a length of DNA that codes for the making of a particular protein.

genetic engineering (modification) the manipulation of genetic material to produce new types of organisms.

genotype the alleles possessed by an organism.

homeostasis maintaining a constant environment for the cells within the body.

intracellular inside cells.

membrane the boundary surrounding all cells and also surrounding organelles within eukaryotic cells. Average thickness 7 nm.

meiosis the type of cell division that results in a halving of chromosome number and a reshuffling of alleles; in humans it occurs in the formation of gametes.

metabolism the chemical reactions taking place in a living organism.

mitochondrion the organelle in eukaryotes in which aerobic respiration takes place. Average diameter 0.7 µm.

mitosis the division of a nucleus such that the two daughter cells acquire exactly the same number and type of chromosomes as the parent cell.

mutation an unpredictable change in the structure of DNA, or in the structure of a number of chromosomes.

nucleus the large membrane-bound organelle in a cell containing DNA for the majority of the cell cycle. Size approximately 7 µm.

nutrient a substance that is required in the diet, e.g. proteins, carbohydrates, fats, vitamins and minerals; water and fibre are not generally regarded as nutrients.

organ a structure within a multicellular organism that is made up of different types of tissues working together to perform a particular function, e.g. the stomach in a human or a leaf in a plant.

organelle a functionally and structurally distinct part of a cell, for example a ribosome or mitochondrion.

osmosis the movement of water molecules from a dilute solution to a concentrated solution, through a partially permeable membrane.

phenotype the characteristics of an organism, often resulting from interactions between its genotype and its environment.

prokaryotic cell a cell that does not contain a nucleus or any other membrane-bound organelles; bacteria are prokaryotes. Average diameter 0.5–5 µm.

receptor a cell which is sensitive to a change in the environment that generates a response as a result of a stimulus.

respiration enzymatic release of energy from organic compounds in living cells.

ribosomes very small organelles (diameter 18–22 µm) found in all cells, where protein molecules are assembled from amino acids.

secretion the release of a useful substance from a cell or gland.

tissue a layer or group of cells of a similar type, which together perform a particular function.

toxin a poison, especially one produced by a pathogen inside the body.

Glossary

amino acids the monomers from which proteins are built; molecules with two functional groups – an amino group and a carboxylic acid group – attached to the same carbon atom.

active site (of an enzyme) the most important region of a functional enzyme; the active site has two functions – it has a structure that recognises and binds the substrate and a catalytic region that helps bring about the reaction catalysed by the enzyme.

amylases enzymes that bring about the breakdown (hydrolysis) of carbohydrates such as starch.

bimolecular layers membranous structures formed by phosphoglycerides (phospholipids) in the presence of water.

carbohydrates compounds containing carbon, hydrogen and oxygen. Carbohydrates include simple sugars such as glucose, disaccharides, and complex polysaccharides such as starch and cellulose.

competitive inhibition a form of enzyme inhibition by molecules that bind to the active site of the enzyme but do not take part in a reaction.

complementary base pairing the basis of how the two helical strands of DNA bond to each other; adenine (A) in one strand is always paired with thymine (T) in the other and cytosine (C) is always paired with guanine (G).

condensation polymerisation a type of polymerisation in which a molecule of water is eliminated each time a monomer molecule is added to the chain; it is used in the building of proteins, nucleic acids and polysaccharides.

denaturation processes by which the complex three-dimensional structure of functional biological molecules such as proteins is destroyed, leading to temporary or permanent loss of activity.

deoxyribonucleic acid (DNA) a double helical polymer which carries the genetic message; each molecule is made up of two anti-parallel polynucleotide chains consisting of a sugar–phosphate backbone with nitrogenous bases attached to them.

disaccharides dimers of two simple sugars joined together by a glycosidic link; maltose and cellobiose are two important disaccharide units as they are the structural units from which the polysaccharides starch and cellulose are assembled.

disulphide bonding a type of covalent bond important in many proteins for maintaining their tertiary and quaternary structure; the bond is formed between the –SH groups of two cysteine residues.

enzymes protein molecules that function as biological catalysts; they are generally more efficient than inorganic catalysts and have a high degree of specificity.

fatty acids long chain carboxylic acids consisting of hydrocarbon chains with a terminal acid group (–COOH); such fatty acids form one of the components of triglycerides and phosphoglycerides.

Fischer projections the standard ways of writing the structures of the straight chain forms of simple sugars so that the spatial arrangement of the groups on each carbon atom is clearly represented.

fluid mosaic model the current model for the structure of cell membranes: a bimolecular layer of phosphoglycerides (phospholipids), with protein molecules embedded in the layer and extending across the bilayer.

glycosidic link the type of bond present in disaccharides and polysaccharides, formed by condensation polymerisation.

glycerol (propan-1,2,3-triol) the molecule central to the structure of triglycerides and phosphoglycerides; the three –OH groups form ester links with the other components of the lipid.

haemoglobin the iron-containing protein found in red blood cells which is responsible for transporting oxygen around the body; it is made up of two α-chains and two β-chains.

hydrogen bonding a type of attraction between molecules which is stronger than other types of inter-molecular force; a hydrogen bond involves a hydrogen atom attached to an electronegative atom (an oxygen or nitrogen atom, for example).

hydrolysis a reaction important in the breakdown of condensation polymers, such as proteins or carbohydrates, in which the elements of water (H and OH) are added to the molecular fragments.

immobilised enzymes enzymes are immobilised by attachment to a solid surface or entrapment within a gel; this can increase both the efficiency of the process and the stability of the enzyme.

lipids compounds grouped together because of their non-polar nature; they tend to be insoluble in water, but soluble in organic solvents such as hexane; biochemically important lipids include triglycerides, phosphoglycerides and steroids.

lipases enzymes responsible for catalysing the breaking of the ester links in triglycerides or phosphoglycerides.

lock-and-key mechanism a model of enzyme activity (first put forward by Fischer) that stresses the importance of molecular shape in explaining the high degree of specificity in enzyme activity.

monosaccharides (simple sugars) molecules with the general formula $(CH_2O)_n$, where n ranges from 3 to 9; glucose, deoxyribose and ribose are biologically important examples.

nitrogenous bases (in DNA and RNA) nitrogen-containing bases involved in the structure of DNA and RNA; in DNA they are adenine (A), guanine (G), thymine (T) and cytosine (C); in RNA uracil (U) replaces thymine.

nucleotides the basic structural units of DNA and RNA; each nucleotide is made from a sugar, deoxyribose or ribose, a phosphate group, and a nitrogen-containing base.

non-competitive inhibition a form of enzyme inhibition in which the inhibitor molecule binds to a region of the enzyme surface other than the active site and thus distorts the shape of the enzyme so that the active site no longer functions.

optical isomerism a form of stereoisomerism shown by molecules that contain a carbon atom with four different groups attached; the isomers are mirror image forms of each other which cannot be superimposed.

peptide bond the link present between amino acids in a polypeptide (protein) chain; the link is formed by a condensation reaction between the amino group ($-NH_2$) of one amino acid and the carboxylic acid group ($-COOH$) of another amino acid.

phosphodiester link a link present in the sugar-phosphate backbone of DNA and RNA strands formed between the $-OH$ groups on the sugar molecules and the intervening phosphate groups.

phosphoglycerides (or phospholipids) the major lipid component of cell membranes; each phosphoglycerides molecule has a polar region or 'head' and a non-polar 'tail'.

primary structure (of proteins) the first of several levels of protein structure; the sequence of amino acids in a polypeptide chain as determined by the gene for that chain.

proteases enzymes which catalyse the breakdown (hydrolysis) of proteins into peptides and amino acids.

proteins condensation polymers of amino acids joined together by peptide bonds; proteins have a range of important functions ranging from structural proteins to enzymes, hormones and antibodies.

quaternary structure (of proteins) the final level of protein structure that applies to proteins that consist of more than one polypeptide chain; deals with how the chains interact to form the functional protein.

replication the process by which new DNA molecules are generated when cells divide, during the process the double helix unwinds and each strand is copied.

ribonucleic acid (RNA) a single-stranded polynucleotide molecule; there are several different types of RNA serving different functions in the mechanism of gene expression.

saponification (soap-making) the alkaline hydrolysis of the triglycerides present in animal fats or vegetable oils to form soap.

secondary structure (of proteins) the second level of protein structure; α-helix and β-pleated sheet, for example, are structures stabilised by hydrogen bonding between peptide bond regions of the polypeptide.

substrate the molecule upon which an enzyme acts to bring about a reaction.

tertiary structure (of proteins) the third level of protein structure involving the overall folding of a polypeptide chain; the chain is stabilised by ionic interactions, van der Waals' forces, hydrogen bonding and covalent disulphide bond formation.

transcription the process in which the genetic message encoded on the template strand of DNA is copied into a messenger RNA (mRNA) molecule.

translation the process by which the message encoded in mRNA is translated into a polypeptide chain by a process involving ribosomes and transfer RNA (tRNA) molecules.

triglycerides (triglyceryl esters) lipids that occur in animal fats and vegetable oils; they are formed by the addition of three long-chain fatty acid molecules to a molecule of glycerol (propan-1,2,3-triol) via ester links.

turnover number a measure of the efficiency of an enzyme – it is the number of substrate molecules reacted per enzyme molecule per minute.

van der Waals' forces weak intermolecular forces that occur between covalent molecules; they occur where weak forces of attraction between dipoles in adjacent molecules result in an interaction.

V_{max} (in saturation kinetics) when the activity of a fixed amount of enzyme is tested with increasing concentrations of substrate, a maximum rate of reaction (Vmax) is reached; the active sites of the enzyme molecules are all occupied by substrate.

Index